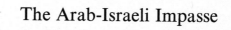

The Arab-Israeli Impasse

THE ARAB-ISRAELI IMPASSE

Expressions of moderate viewpoints on the
Arab-Israeli conflict by well known
western writers.

Editor: Majdia D. Khadduri

ROBERT B. LUCE, INC.
WASHINGTON

EDITOR'S FOREWORD

The Middle East crisis, though its significance is clearly becoming global, has been narrowly viewed by many observers as merely a conflict between Israel and her immediate Arab neighbors, especially Egypt, Syria and Jordan. In reality the issue goes deeper and wider into a region extending from the Atlantic to the Indian oceans and inhabited by more than one hundred million people. It includes the whole of North Africa, the Arab crescent comprising the area between the Mediterranean and the Persian Gulf, and the Arabian Peninsula. These countries, though often differing on certain matters of local interest, are united in their defense of Arab rights against Israel. Because of the religious affinity between Arabs and Muslims in Asia and Africa, the four hundred million Muslims of these continents are now showing increasing concern about Israel's resort to force in imposing her demands on the Arabs without regard to their rights and feelings.

No sooner had the crisis arisen in May 1967 than books and periodical material began to make their appearance in an increasing quantity to explain its nature and possible consequences. Unfortunately the bulk of published accounts has either explained or expounded the Israeli viewpoint on the subject without regard to the rights and grievances of the other party (or parties) concerned. Little has been written with detachment which might throw light on the deeper causes of the conflict and its adverse effects on Western prestige and interests in that part of the world. As a result, an objective discussion of the issue has been palpably lacking and no balanced assessment of the conflict has yet been presented to the public. It is the purpose of this editor to put together in a single volume the views of a few writers well-known for their moderation, long experience and fair-mindedness, which may help the reader to form a more balanced opinion on the nature and ramifications of the conflict.

The Editor wishes to acknowledge the kindnesses of all the writers and publishers who have given permission to reproduce their published material in this volume. Needless to say, she alone is responsible for any error that may have been made in editing these papers.

M. D. K.

May 31, 1968
Washington, D. C.

CONTENTS

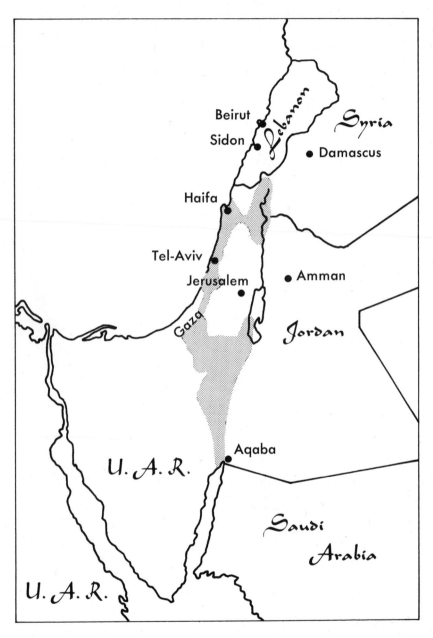

United Nations 1947 Partition Plan for Israel

They were concerned with the presentation of their own point of view in the particular magazine that had opened its columns to them. Each piece has been written by someone who having studied Middle East problems at first hand, has come not only to feel a very deep respect and affection for the Arabs but to recognize that they have been the victims of bad faith at the hands of their western neighbours.

Myself in late September 1941, I was posted as liaison officer with the rank of Captain to General Spears' military mission to Syria and the Lebanon. Britain's fortunes were then at their lowest ebb, but we had enjoyed a minor success in the Levant. We had defeated a pro-nazi *coup d'etat* in Iraq and in concert with General de Gaulle's Free French Forces had dispossessed the Vichy government of its hold on Syria and the Lebanon.

My duties were explained to me on my arrival in Beirut. I must do all I could to maintain friendly relations with the French and to assist them in their management of the country. The French were distrustful of the British; they thought that we had designs on Syria and the Lebanon. A few years earlier Pierre Benoit had in his novel "La Chatelaine du Liban" used as his villain, a deviously intentioned British intelligence officer in Palestine. That book presented a point of view that it was a part of my duty to confute. The French had to be convinced that as soon as the war was over we would retire behind our own frontiers. I was also encouraged to mix as much as possible with the Lebanese and in the process remind them how fortunate they were to be protected by French arms and to have their spirits sustained by the cultural influence of France. The Lebanese were not, it seemed, particularly appreciative of their good fortune. Their country had been fought over; their cities had been bombed; several years earlier they had been promised their independence, but the promises had not been implemented. I must be careful, I was adjured, to say nothing critical of the French. Amicable relations must be maintained so that as few troops as possible would be needed here, leaving our generals free to concentrate upon our main objective—the defeat of the Germans in the field. Everything was secondary to that.

10

I spent six months in Beirut. It was a happy time. The Lebanon is a charming country and the Lebanese are a delightful people—gay, charming, witty, international with a very real culture of their own, and an air of frivolity that is belied by a sound business sense. I soon realized that they were not much interested in the war. There had been so many wars. Their narrow strip of coast had been over-run by so many conquerors—Phoenicians, Greeks, Romans, Turks. They could not defend themselves. They shrugged their shoulders, compromised with necessity and made their 1%.

From Beirut I went to Cairo. I did not much like it there. The atmosphere was uncongenial. The British were not popular. Their relations with the court were bad. A few months earlier, the Royal Palace had been surrounded with tanks. An ultimatum had been delivered to the King. He must abdicate or appoint the Prime Minister the British favoured. We were there on sufferance. A large part of the population was eager to welcome the German and Italian forces.

It was a relief to get away from Cairo. I was posted to Syria, to Deraa, the base of T. E. Lawrence's activities. I was in charge of a section of the Wheat Commission. The British and French were organizing the distribution of the harvest, and the landowners were not anxious to sell. They doubted if the allies were winning the war. They wanted to hoard as much of their wheat as possible. They did not trust the paper money that was backed by France. They would have preferred to be paid in gold. Yet they were reasonable enough. They knew that they had to make a deal with the occupying forces: it was a question of how much they could manage to retain. It was an occasion for diplomacy.

The seven weeks I spent there were my real introduction to the Arab World. The Beirutis and Cairenes had been Westernized, but the Sheikhs of the Hauran were part of the long tradition of the desert for which Mohammed had drawn up his edicts. I was now seeing the Arabs in their own villages, in their own homes. I was accompanied by an interpreter. Squatted on a cushion, I would deliberate for hour after hour, the problems of their store of wheat. At appropriate intervals I would be invited to sip their strong and bitter coffee. Children would peer through the doorway at us. Senior members of the community would join us, would pay their respects 'to the headman—the mouktar—would listen to the long discussions, then when they had satisfied their curiosity take their leave. It was both formal and informal. There was an atmosphere of importance, but none of hurry. It is bad manners in the Arab World to be in a hurry. Invariably a meal of some kind would be served, chicken or a sheep. The mouktar would seat me at his side. We would eat with our fingers. He would select from the steaming dish the most succulent morsels for my delectation. It was all a part of the immemorial traditions of the Arab World. I came during those weeks to appreciate the dignity and basic human feeling of that world. But I learnt more than that. I learnt that that world had no part whatever in our quarrel with the Germans. It was not their war. They were unconcerned with the western conception of democracy that was, so we claimed, at stake. They were only concerned with the preservation of their own traditions and their own way of life.

From the Hauran I was posted to Baghdad where I worked in counter espionage until the end of the war—a period of thirty months. In 1914, Iraq had consisted of the three villayets of Mosul, Basra and Baghdad. Like the individual states of the Union of the United States they had been separate entities in the Ottoman Empire, equal under the Bureaucracy of Constantinople. The merchants of Baghdad had had easy access to their cousins in Damascus and Beirut. Many Baghdadis went north to Constantinople for their education. Quite a few joined the Turkish army, Nuri Sa'id for example. In principle the Ottoman Empire presented a workable solution for the problems of the Middle East, but its bureaucracy had become brutal, corrupt, and inefficient. And there was among the Arabs a mounting spirit of nationalism, of revolt against their Turkish overlords, very similar to that which at the close of the eighteenth century had fired the Spanish colonies of Central and South America against the domination of Seville. There is a close parallel between the two situations and if had there been no intervention of Providence, the Mesopotamian villayets would during the 1920's and the 1930's have broken loose from Turkey, in the same way that Colombia, Peru, Chile and Argentina broke loose from Spain.

Fate did intervene, however, when war broke out between Germany and England, Turkey joined the German side, and Britain decided to foment the Arab spirit of revolt, arming and financing it and promising the Arabs independence when victory had been achieved. Victory was achieved but the promises were not kept, and the Arab world was divided into separate countries as protectorates under the tutelage of France and Britain; while the Balfour Declaration sponsored the creation in Palestine of a national home for the Jews, provided that this home did not interfere with the rights and liberties of the existing residents. At that time a bare nine per cent of the population of Palestine was Jewish, and relations between Jews and Arabs were generally cordial; there as elsewhere in the Arab World.

In August 1914, the weekly paper John Bull placarded England with the announcement of an article by H. G. Wells, entitled "The War that will end War." In 1919 cynics were describing the Treaty of Versailles as "The Peace that will end Peace." As regards the Arab World that was an accurate definition of that treaty.

Several of the essays in this book have charted the graph of the subsequent slow descent towards the present chaos. Britain as her share of the package deal got the mandates of Palestine and Iraq, and not without a sense of guilt at her failure to implement the promises that had been made on her behalf by Lawrence, did her best to carry out honestly and honorably the terms of her protectorates. By 1930 Iraq was an independent sovereign state with an established monarchy. Admittedly it was a sphere of British influence, with a military mission, an air base at Habbaniya and treaty rights for the Port of Basra. A number of technical advisers were appointed to the various ministries. In a sense we still ran the country, but the technical advisers were first class men, who recognized that their first duty was to make their posts obsolete. There was no attempt made as there was by

13

the French in Syria and Lebanon to turn a protectorate into a colony. We did our best but it was all too late.

My own assignment as a security officer in Baghdad during 1943 and 1944 was a simple but not unimportant one. The tide of the war had turned. Mesopotamia had ceased to provide a fighting front; but it was even so of great strategic value as the line of communication by which aid was sent to Russia through the Persian Gulf, and by which oil was shipped to Europe. It was of first importance that the lines of communication should be kept clear and that in the process the minimum number of fighting troops should be employed. Once again Arabs had become involved in a war that was no concern of theirs.

One has to take a short view in war time, with the enemy at the gates, one has to use the weapons that lie to hand. In 1943 just as in 1916 Britain had only one objective, to defeat Germany as quietly and expeditiously as possible. Yet as I sat in my office on the banks of the broad brown Tigris, that had reflected once the domes and minarets of the Caliphs, I could not help wondering what would be happening here in fifteen years time, when the British troops had retired and with the Regency at an end the young King had to work out his own destiny. We all knew what legacy Britain's quarrel with Germany in 1914 had handed to the Arab World; what legacy would be handed over as a result of this new quarrel, quarter of a century later.

The essays in this book describe and analyze the nature of those legacies. Most of them having diagnosed the malady, suggest a cure. I do not myself see any immediate therapy for that festering sore and I do not see how the Western world can fail to become involved in its outcome. I can only hope that those who are responsible for this involvement will take to heart the message that these essays contain. Let them always remember that these troubles have arisen because the west involved the Arab World in their disputes. Had the Arabs been left to themselves they would have worked out their troubles peacefully.

INTRODUCTION
Quincy Wright

Majdia Khadduri has performed a valuable service in collecting articles offering a variety of points of view on the Middle Eastern problem and particularly on the six day war of June 1967. Articles of both historical and evaluative character are included. The Arab position, misunderstood in the United States, is presented in several of the articles.

The background of the present situation is presented with considerable variations in emphasis by three distinguished diplomats and historians. Sir John Glubb, former adviser to the government of Jordan, emphasizes the strategic importance of the Middle East in promoting or blocking trade between East and West in ancient and modern history, indicated by the efforts of Napoleon in 1798 and of Winston Churchill in 1941 to control Egypt when the strategic situation nearer home seemed desperate. He believes that competition between the Soviet Union and the West to dominate the area lay behind the hostilities of June, 1967. He also notes the contribution of the Arabs in bringing the mathematical, scientific and philosophical knowledge of the East to Europe during the Middle Ages. Arnold Toynbee, distinguished world historian, objectively states the positions of Israel and of the Arabs, both grounded in remote history, and his own position appreciative of both but emphasizing the need of compromise. While Sir John Glubb attributes much responsibility for the recent war to the Soviet Union, Toynbee notes the role of British, German, and United States policies in developing an explosive situation in the area since World War I. Anthony Nutting, former British Minister of State, agrees with many Arabs in perceiving the Balfour Declaration of 1917, in conflict with the McMahon agreements of 1915, as the origin of the tragedy. Israel, he thinks, will not disappear from Palestine as the Crusaders did after two centuries, so both Arabs and Jews must eventually accept a bi-national state.

These writers all recognize the contribution which the Arabs have made to civilization and suggest an answer to the questions: Who are the Arabs? and What are the Arab countries? Although all Arabs understand the language of the Qur'an they speak it in different dialects. They are for the most part Muslim but among them are different Muslim sects and some Christians especially in Lebanon. The one hundred million Arabs constitute a minority of about four hundred million Moslems in the world. The Arabs are a people of considerable racial, cultural and political diversity in thirteen states—Iraq, Kuwait, Saudi Arabia, Yemen, Syria, Lebanon, Jordan, Egypt, Sudan, Libya, Tunisia, Algeria, Morocco—in the Middle East and North Africa. As Sir John Glubb emphasizes, some Arabs think that they can gain from close relations with the Soviet Union, others prefer close relations with the West. Their views on solution of the Palestine problem also vary considerably although, as members of the Arab League, they are united in opposition to Israel which they accuse of illegal penetration into an area which had been Arab for centuries, of expelling many Palestinian Arabs from their homes and of pursuing a policy of imperialistic expansion by armed force.

Albert Hourani, in presenting the Arab position, notes that there is no hostility between Arabs and Jews as people but the Arabs will not accept political Zionism. The British policy of a bi-national state in Palestine failed because of

the immigration issue. The issue concerning territorial boundaries and human dignity for the refugees must, he thinks,
be settled.

In addition to the position of the Arabs, the position of
the Powers and the United States are presented. The course
of events leading to the six day war is narrated in detail by
Charles W. Yost, former United States delegate to the
United Nations. He emphasizes the Egyptian belief, perhaps
stimulated by Soviet information, that Israel was about to
attack Syria, but he thinks that neither Egypt nor Israel
wanted war. He blames the Great Powers and the United
Nations, as well as the Arabs and Israel, for their "failure
to face the facts of life in the Middle East during the twenty
years," before June 1967, and exhorts the Arabs and Israel
to learn the art of "peaceful coexistence." John Badeau,
former United States Ambassador to Egypt, emphasizes the
role of false images, misinformation, and miscalculation in the
action of both Israel and Egypt. Among the Arabs, a loqua-
cious people, words do not necessarily mean action, while
among the Israeli words and action are more closely related,
but neither understood this before the crisis. Americans, in
Ambassador Badeau's opinion, do not generally understand
the Arab point of view and neither the Arabs nor the
Soviet Union understand the Americans.

An article by a reporter attributing the information to a
high Soviet functionary is reprinted from a French leftist
periodical. It presents an interesting account of Soviet policy
and mistakes, before and during the crisis and predicts future
policies. The Soviets, according to the article, persuaded
Nasser to take measures to prevent Israel from invading Syria
which they believed imminent. Nasser made a mistake, in
Soviet opinion, in demanding withdrawal of UNEF from his
frontiers with Israel and in blockading the Gulf of Aqaba.
After hostilities began, the Soviets utilized the "hot line" to
the United States to prevent their escalation. The Soviets were
mistaken about Egyptian military capability and Nasser was
mistaken in thinking the United States would restrain Israel
which they considered an American puppet. As the war pro-
gressed, some Soviet leaders favored direct help to Egypt but
the United States and Jewish opinion in Russia dissuaded the

government from such a policy. The article predicted that Soviet policy of opposing "Israel imperialism" would be tougher after the war.

Don Cordtz, Elmer Berger, and Jean LaCouture comment on United States policy in the Middle East in a pessimistic vein. Cordtz emphasizes the rapid deterioration of the image of the United States in the Arab world in recent years and the difficulty, encountered by the United States in attempting to maintain impartiality in the Middle Eastern conflict. He calls for a reconsideration of American policy in the area.

Harry N. Howard, formerly in the State Department, points out that the Arabs have been willing to accept the boundaries of Israel in the original United Nations resolution of November 1947, and emphasizes, as does Hourani, the need for agreement on boundaries and refugees. He discusses the work of UNRWA, the largest U.N. subsidiary agency with a staff of 11,600 mostly Palestinian refugees, and an annual budget of $37,000,000. The diversity of attitudes among American Christians during the war is discussed critically by Willard G. Oxtoby and the resolution of the National Council of Churches in July 1967, is printed in the collection. The latter supports the policy of mutual concession recommended by the resolution of the U.N. Security Council in November 1967, also printed.

The selection of articles brings out the differences in interpretation of facts and in appraisal of proposed solutions indicating the difficulty of ending the conflict which has led to three wars since the partition of Palestine in 1947. Most of the writers are pessimistic but the reader can deduce the need for solutions which will seem just to both Arabs and Israelis and will, therefore, relax tensions, promote stability, and preserve peace in the Middle East.

1.

THE BACKGROUND

Foreign Office,
November 2nd, 1917

Dear Lord Rothschild,

I have much pleasure in conveying to you, on behalf of His Majesty's Government, the following declaration of sympathy with Jewish Zionist aspirations which has been submitted to, and approved by, the Cabinet.

"His Majesty's Government views with favour the establishment in Palestine of a national home for the Jewish people, and will use their best endeavors to facilitate the achievement of this object, it being clearly understood that nothing shall be done which may prejudice the civil and religious rights of existing non-Jewish communities in Palestine, or the rights and political status enjoyed by Jews in any other country."

I should be grateful if you would bring this declaration to the knowledge of the Zionist Federation.

Yours,

A. W. James Balfour

Lieut. Gen. Sir John Bagot Glubb was educated at Cheltenham and Royal Military Academy, Woolwich. His outstanding military career in the Middle East culminated in his assuming command of the Jordanian Arab Legion (1938-1956). Among the many books he has authored are "Story of the Arab Legion," "Britain and the Arabs," and "The Great Arab Conquests."

Address delivered to the Middle East Institute, October 26, 1967, Washington, D. C.

THE MIDDLE EAST SITUATION
Sir John Bagot Glubb

I don't know if you know the story of the two old ladies who came out of their houses into their back yards one morning and they saw each other over the fence. One said to the other, "Good morning, Mrs. Jones. How are you this morning? You are looking rather worried; nothing wrong, I hope." So the other one said, "Well, yes, I am. I am real worried, Mrs. Smith. I sent my husband out yesterday afternoon to buy a cabbage for our dinner today, and he hasn't come back. He has been out all night." So the first one said, "Oh, I shouldn't worry about that, dear, if he doesn't come back, you can always open a can of peas."

You see the point is that these two ladies were both confronted with the same situation but their reactions were different regarding the important element in this situation. What I want to try and do this evening is to present to you a point of view regarding recent events in the Middle East, which is not identical, I think, with the one which is usually represented in the press.

History as we know it began 5,000 or so years ago. And in the intervening period, quite a lot of nations have succeeded one another as the dominant power of their time. You can start way back with the Pharaohs, the Assyrians, the Babylonians, the Ancient Persians, Alexander the Great, and the Greeks, the Romans, the Arabs, the Ottomans, and even the British.

That pretty well covers the so-called empires of the past except the Spaniards who did it over here; but otherwise, there is a curious, single factor which all these empires in history for 5,000 years have shared, and that is every single one of those held Egypt. Now this seems rather striking when you think of it—they were in all sorts of different parts of the world—but every one of them made a bee-line for Egypt as soon as they could. And I think if we analyze this, we can find very good reasons for their choice. The first is, of course, if you visualize a map of the old world, that Egypt and the Middle East are the only passageway connecting Europe and the Mediterranean with the Indian Ocean, India, the Far East, Indonesia, and Australia.

Secondly, if again you visualize the old world, omitting China perhaps, which always led its own life, the Middle East is exactly the center of the continents of Europe, Asia and Africa. It is also the only land connection between these three continents. And, as a result, any great power at any period of history which held Egypt was able itself either to move into Europe, Asia or Africa, or conversely and perhaps at times even more important, by, so-to-speak, establishing a roadblock at this crossroads they could prevent anybody else from going to any other place.

Now it takes a bit too long this evening to start 5,000 years ago, so I am going to start in the 7th Century after Christ. At that time the world was divided into two halves, much as it is today—an eastern and a western power bloc. The western bloc was the Roman Empire, and the eastern bloc was the Persian Empire, and the border between the two was almost exactly along the frontier between Syria and Iraq today. And you will remember, that immediately south of that frontier lies the Peninsula of Arabia. This peninsula in the 7th Century—it's mostly desert—was inhabited by a number of nomadic tribes who were looked down upon with some contempt by the inhabitants of these old and cultured empires.

There is only one other point worth noting here and that is that the Roman Empire included all the frontiers, all the shores of the Mediterranean and so, many countries which we consider oriental—such as Turkey today, Syria, Palestine, Egypt, what we call Tunisia, Algeria, Morocco—were until the 7th Century, you might say, part of Europe. Their official languages were Greek and Latin, and the inhabitants were Christians.

Mohammed was born in 570 A.D. down in this desert peninsula. He began to preach in 614 and he died in 632. Two years after his death, these despised and backward nomads suddenly broke out of their desert peninsula; towards the east they completely eliminated the Persian Empire, crossed what we now call Afghanistan, and over into the plains of northern India. Another lot went further to the left or north, up into what is now Soviet territory, north of Tibet until they came to the frontiers of China.

Anybody with any sense, of course, when the world is divided into two power blocs, if he wants to attack one power bloc, makes friends with the other. But the Arabs didn't do this; they attacked both the power blocs at once. While half of them were going east in this direction, the other half were going west. They quickly overran Syria, Palestine and Egypt, across North Africa to Morocco, over the Straits of Gibraltar, up through France, and, I am glad to say, they eventually stopped 250 miles from the coast of England. Within the life-time of one man, these people who had no education, no technology, no particular government, no form of organization, you might almost say, defeated both the world power blocs and established an empire which extended from the Atlantic Ocean to the borders of China.

Now the curious part about this fantastic conquest is the small number of men who carried it out. Nearly all of these countries were conquered by armies of 12-15,000 men. And the result was that when this immense empire had been conquered, it has been estimated that Arabs constituted around 1% of the inhabitants of the territory which they had conquered. The remainder was populated by all sorts of different races—South of France was in there first, Spain, people from North Germany such as the Goths and the

Vandals, Berbers in North Africa, Egyptians, Syrians, Greeks, Armenians, Persians, Turks, Indians—14 or 15 utterly different ethnic races were all involved in this empire.

I think this is of tremendous significance today. We are sometimes told by propaganda that anybody from Morocco to Persia is now an Arab, and of course, anybody can call himself anything he likes if he wants to. But we are apt to conclude from this that this is a homogeneous ethnic group, extending from Morocco to Persia. This is completely illusory. In fact, they are all entirely different nations, very often with quite contradictory qualities. Fortunately we still have in the original a report written by the Arab Governor of Turkestan which is now in Soviet Russia, to the Caliph in Damascus, 75 years after the Arabs broke out of Arabia. And in his letter, he says, there have been so many conversions to Islam during the past year that if things go on this way, very soon everybody in this country will be an "Arab."

This is a very natural, you see, mixup. The idea of Arab was associated with the Muslim religion, and easily enough, anybody who became a Muslim (in fact, many of them did it for this reason—the Arabs enjoyed so much prestige after their conquests) that anybody, whatever his origin—although he might be from North Germany—when he adopted the Moslem religion, claimed to be a member of the conquering race.

In fact, it always seems to me that Latin America is probably the nearest parallel. There everybody speaks Spanish and they are all Roman Catholics. But they are not Spaniards. Just as in the case of the Arab countries of today, they acquired their language and their religion from a military conquest many centuries ago.

In the 8th, 9th and 10th centuries, the relative positions of this Arab Empire and of Europe were just about the opposite of what they are today. Everything that we connect with ourselves belonged to them. Everything we attribute to them belonged to us. For example, such things as industry, banking, science, education, shipping, commerce, naval command of the sea, all these things were a monopoly of the Arab Empire. If you lived in Europe, when you wanted a

24

manufactured article you had to import it from some Arab country. So complete was their naval command of the Mediterranean and the Red Sea, that a contemporary writer said, no Christian can any longer so much as float a wooden plank on the Mediterranean.

This complete domination of the world as it then was lasted for 250 years. In between brackets that's exactly the same time the British Empire lasted. After 250 years it broke up into separate segments, but even so, Spain, Morocco, to Turkestan and Northern India were still all Muslim states. After the loss of their political domination, they remained the intellectual leaders for another 250 years. And I think they may well be called the pioneers of modern science, because they introduced to us our method of writing numbers, which we still, incidentally, call Arabic numerals, namely having units, tens, hundreds and thousands, next door to one another. The Romans, you will remember, used to write a thing like MM, CC, LXXX, VVV, III. How anybody added or subtracted that, much less divided or multiplied, I have never found out.

Anyhow, by introducing this method of numerical notation, they laid the foundation of our mathematics. Although I lived with them for 36 years, I always had a sneaking resentment against the Arabs because they went on from that to invent logarithms, algebra and trigonometry.

For many centuries they were the leaders of the world in medicine, ophthalmology, chemistry, zoology and all the minor sciences. Among other things, they introduced to Europe rhyming poetry. Again the Greeks and the Latins, you may remember, used to scan their lines, but the final syllable didn't rhyme. As the result of Arab influence, our poetry has sounded quite nice since then—until quite recently.

They also introduced to Europe the manufacture of paper, and to be perfectly candid, they didn't invent this, the Chinese did; but as the boundaries of the Moslem Empire extended from China to Spain, they brought the manufacture of paper to Europe. They actually accurately measured the circumference of the earth 600 years before Europe got around to admitting the darned thing wasn't flat.

Now the interesting thing about this period is what happened to Europe while all this was going on. The Roman community was very similar to our own. It was a commercial and a capitalist society. The big men were business men and bankers. The cities dominated the country-side and they maintained active overseas commerce with India and China and were, of course, enabled to do this because the Romans held Egypt and had a fleet on the Red Sea as well as on the Mediterranean. But as soon as the Arabs interposed this long line of country from Morocco over to China, along the south of Europe, Europe found itself suddenly cut off from all overseas commerce. Of course, America and the Cape of Good Hope had not been discovered, and within a few years this prosperous financial society withered away. For around five centuries Europe became an agricultural community. There was no money, all they did was they grew their own food and from the wool of their sheep they manufactured their own clothing.

Where there is no money, land becomes the standard of wealth instead of cash. When the bankers disappeared, the barons became the leaders, and, I think it is a sobering thought to remember that until the beginning of this very century in which we are living—until after I was actually born—in western Europe, land owners were considered socially superior to businessmen; that is, that this 500-year old Moslem blockade of Europe distorted the social development of Europe for something like 12 centuries.

I can't help feeling—at least this is what happened to me—that knowledge of this period changed the whole of my outlook on life. When I was at school I suffered a certain amount about the Greeks and the Romans, but after that, we went on to William the Conquerer and the conquest of England, and I must admit when I was a school boy I didn't even notice that 800 years had been missed out. But when you discover those 800 years, especially if you live in the Middle East where the remains of them are visible every day, you suddenly get a new outlook on history.

Of the 5,000 years of history we can trace, for 4,500 years Syria and Egypt were in the leadership of human progress. It is only in the last 500 years that we in the West have not only caught up but now out-distance them. And I must say it sort of made a philosophical change in my thought. Of course, like everybody else, I had always assumed that the western races were so superior to the other poor chaps who happened to be around in this world that they weren't in anything like the same category. And to find out that both the Romans and the Arabs during the centuries of their predominance had been just as brilliant, just as powerful, just as far ahead of everybody else, as the western European and North American peoples are now, just as absolutely convinced of their natural superiority—which, of course, they assumed would last till the day of resurrection— made me think again about our own vast superiority over everybody else.

Now some people say to me "Now this can't be true because I have never heard about it before." I think this is the most masterly piece of censorship that is recorded in history. And the only explanation you can get is that for that 500 years Europe had been blockaded, her prosperity had withered away, and she had lived in continual fear of invasion or attack from North Africa or from the Middle East.

After the conquests I have already outlined, the Arabs went on to occupy the Balearic Islands, Corsica, Sardinia, Sicily, southern Italy, Crete. They landed in Rome and burned St. Peter's. They landed frequently in northern Italy and they had complete command of the Mediterranean. And it does appear as if when Europe eventually overtook and passed them, and the Renaissance got in full swing, they tacitly agreed that the least said about the previous period, the better.

This Arab culture which lead the world for so many centuries concluded in 1055. It happens to be the date on which the Seljuk Turks captured Baghdad. From then onwards, a whole stream of disasters ensued. The Seljuks were not too bad in the end, but then came the Mongols, and you have all heard of Genghis Khan, Hulagu, Tamerlane, and people of that kind. Their policy was, whenever they came to a city, not only to destroy it, burn it and plow it up, but to collect all the inhabitants of the city regardless of age or sex and murder them on a plain outside.

27

The Mongols were followed by the Mamelukes who were also Turks and then the Ottomans. But an interesting factor to this is that these Central Asian barbarians did not get to Egypt or across North Africa, and this highly cultured Arab civilization remained unadulterated, one might almost say, in Spain and Sicily and the fringes of Southern Europe. And as they weakened it was from them that Europe once again learned civilization, culture and the high standard of living.

But even though the Europeans acquired a certain amount of civilization from these outposts, Europe was still blockaded. It was only just before 1500 that the turning point came.

In 1492 Columbus discovered America and five years later, in 1497, Vasco da Gama sailed around the Cape of Good Hope. All of a sudden, within five years, Europe which had been blockaded for 600 years found the oceans of the world open to her. Not only so, but the Europeans quickly nipped around the Cape of Good Hope and obtained naval command of the Indian Ocean—first the Portuguese, then the Dutch and afterwards the English. And from the Indian Ocean they sailed back up the Red Sea, and whereas the holders of Egypt had always enjoyed all the free commerce with the East, Egypt and the Muslim countries now found themselves in turn blockaded by Europeans so that they couldn't trade, and this put the whole situation into reverse. The Dark Ages of Europe came to an end, and the Dark Ages of the Middle East began.

So if we take this year 1500—it's an easy one to remember—three years after the Cape of Good Hope was discovered—we may take that as the turning point. On top of that, in 1517, Syria and Egypt were conquered by the Ottoman Turks. I think it's worth noticing that the long period of the Dark Ages of Europe, during which the Arabs were enjoying their brilliant period, and the reverse—the commencement of the Middle Ages (the Dark Ages of the Middle East) during which Europe enjoyed predominance—were switched across merely by the blocking and the opening of a trade route.

From 1500 to nearly 1800, three hundred years, the

oceans of the world were covered with ships. Europe was forging far ahead, and the Muslim countries were blockaded on the Mediterranean side and in the Red Sea. From being, since the beginning of history, the center of human progress, Egypt, Syria and the neighboring countries became complete backwaters.

The first man who seems to have looked at the map and realized how important this area was, was Napoleon Bonaparte. You may remember in 1798 France was at war with practically the whole of Europe. Napoleon was just commencing his career, but instead of driving back the enemies of France he took a chance on it; he put his army onto ships, crossed the Mediterranean, and occupied Egypt. And his plan was to establish a French base in Egypt, to hold command of the Mediterranean, and to build a French fleet on the Red Sea. And he reckoned that a French fleet in the Red Sea, based on Egypt, would be able to snatch naval command of the Indian Ocean from the English, whose fleet was maintained by the far more distant route round the Cape of Good Hope. He made a slight miscalculation because while he was occupying Egypt he left his fleet moored in the mouth of the Nile, and Lord Nelson came in and destroyed it. And this spoiled the whole plan. Napoleon was cut off from France, the campaign was abandoned, and he had to go back home. But in the last years of his life, when he was in St. Helena and when he was dictating his memoirs, one of the things he emphasized was that his career had been changed by his failure to hold the Middle East. And on a different occasion, to the Governor of St. Helena, Sir Hudson Lowe, he said, "The great thing to remember is that Egypt is the most important country in the world."

The Napoleonic debacle resulted in a period of confusion in Egypt. The Ottomans had lost their grip, so they sent a force of Albanians, commanded by one Mohammed Ali, to tidy up Egypt for them. Mohammed Ali and the Albanians tidied the place up all right, but they didn't do it for the Ottomans. Mohammed Ali kept it for himself, and as you know, his descendants ruled Egypt until 1952.

This is extremely relevant to the present situation, because Mohammed Ali, although a Muslim, was a European, born on the border of Macedonia and Albania. And he was the first ruler of the Middle East who introduced European officers and European technicians. His army was trained by French officers, and he also brought in doctors, engineers, and other similar experts. This gave Egypt a hundred years' lead on the other Arab countries which were still occupied by the Ottomans. People often say to me, "Of course, Egyptians are the traditional leaders of the Arabs." But this, as a matter of fact, is an illusion. During the great days of the Arabs, their first capital was at Medina, in the Peninsula; the next one was in Damascus, and the third one was in Baghdad.

Mohammed Ali's grandson, Khedive Ismail, was an even more enthusiastic westernizer than Mohammed Ali himself. He boasted that he had made Egypt a part of Europe. Egypt was covered with railways, telegraphs, harbors, even a French opera house in Cairo. The unfortunate part was that you couldn't in those days travel first and pay afterwards. He did it all on credit, and that wasn't so fashionable then as it is now, and after a bit, the creditors began asking for some money or at least some interest, and when he couldn't pay, Khedive Ismail went bankrupt.

To begin with, Britain and France established a financial commission and afterwards the French fell out and Britain took over alone. But before this happened, Ismail had made one of the big reversals of history. In 1869 he opened the Suez Canal. As I said before, from 1500 onwards, Egypt had been a backwater. It is true, it was increasingly used for passenger traffic—they got off at Alexandria and rode across the Suez where they got onto another ship. The East India Company used to use it for urgent dispatches or valuable stores or something of this kind, but the main route of commerce was round the Cape. From 1869 onwards, everybody could see what only Napoleon had seen before, that Egypt was once again the most important country in the world.

Throughout the ensuing period, until World War I, Britain was the country with the biggest stake in this passageway through the Middle East, because she was the biggest maritime, commercial power. Everybody in Western Europe was involved in it, but Britain more than the others. We mustn't forget, of course, that some of the most active maritime peoples in Western Europe are the Dutch, the Danes, the Norwegians, and the Swedes—and all these West European peoples were deeply concerned in the Suez Canal.

The policy adopted by Britain throughout the nineteenth century was to prop up the Ottoman Empire in order to keep another great power from getting astride of the trade route. She was assisted on all sorts of different occasions by the other powers of Western Europe. In the Crimean War, for example, Italy and France joined. During the nineteenth century there were I think, eleven different wars between Russia and the Ottoman Empire, Russia trying to get down to the Mediterranean and to the Middle East passageway. In most or all of these, the powers of Western Europe intervened to support the Ottomans, sometimes Austria-Hungary came in, sometimes Germany came in, nearly always Britain and France were involved—because this was the lifeline of Western Europe.

I may perhaps interject a note here, that neither Russia nor the United States use this passageway to any vital extent. Russia, of course, has land connections with Asia, and unfortunately the United States is exactly the opposite side of the globe. So if from America people want to get to the Indian Ocean, it's quicker for them to go across the Pacific than it is across the Atlantic, the Mediterranean, and through the Middle East defile.

When World War I came, this traditional policy was all of a sudden destroyed. The Ottomans joined the Germans, and in 1914 and '15 a Turko-German force actually reached the banks of the Suez Canal. The British were obliged to detach a large army from the defense of the West and send it to Egypt where it gradually pushed the Germans and the Ottomans back up through Palestine to Syria. When the war was over, however, Britain was faced with the problem of how to continue her traditional policy which was to support the local government, whatever it might be, in order to keep out major powers which were on the same level as herself. These were either Russia or Germany. Nobody had ever been afraid that the Ottomans would try and block it, and so Britain had the idea that, "Why not let the Arabs be independent governments—or a government—in this area and we will behave with them as we behaved to the Ottomans, letting them run their own show and propping them up if Russia or Germany appear on the horizon."

This, during World War I, appeared also to be the best thing for the Arabs themselves. They had been ruled by the Ottomans for 400 years, and to recreate national government required the assistance of somebody from outside. In 1917, however, the British Government issued the Balfour Declaration.

Now this is extremely interesting because you see here a contradiction of policies. We have to remember that in 1917 Russia made peace with Germany and Austria-Hungary, and in the autumn of 1917 Britain and France realized that in the spring of 1918 all the Central Powers would turn on them. And this was the absolute crisis of the war. Even as things worked out, as you know, in April and May 1918 there was nothing to choose—it might have gone any way at a moment's notice. And so in the autumn of 1917 they decided that something must be done to get the United States into the war before they were exhausted. And from the documents which we now have available we see that it was thought that the Balfour Declaration would bring the United States into the war. Now this is very interesting because you see here two policies, one the traditional policy, more than 100 years old, of propping up the local government, and another, a short term policy of trying to save themselves from defeat by a conflicting promise.

After the war, the French also insisted on directly governing Syria, which was not in the original plan and so the traditional policy of supporting the Arabs in order to put something up against the Germans or the Russians was partly vitiated by these two diversions. The French didn't allow the Arabs in Syria to have their independent state, and Zionist immigration began into Palestine.

It's interesting to look back now to the beginning of World War II, when in 1940 and '41 Britain was fighting alone against the whole of Europe, exactly the way France had been in 1798. And Winston Churchill, exactly like Napoleon Bonaparte, although Britain was threatened with invasion across the Channel, loaded a British army onto the sea, sent it around the Cape of Good Hope, and told it to hang on to Egypt whatever happened. Both these are the greatest—or some of the greatest—strategic experts that the world has seen, and under precisely similar circumstances they both decided to risk the safety of their own countries in order to hold on to Egypt.

As you remember, in World War II the tide turned when the Western powers not only held Egypt but occupied North Africa. As soon as the American and British armies held the whole of North Africa it was all over but the shouting.

When the war was over the British Government made another bid to revive their traditional policy. They got, I think, seven Arab governments together—it might be nine, I can't remember offhand—and persuaded them to form a thing called the Arab League. People have expressed various opinions, firstly, "The British were fools, why did they do it?" and secondly, "The British were doublecrossing everybody else." But in actual fact, this is a perfectly obvious move.

The one thing they were longing to do all the time was to get some kind of a local set-up which would look after these countries and with a certain amount of assistance from Western Europe would be able to keep major powers from straddling the Middle East causeway. They also succeeded in persuading or hustling or pushing the French out of Syria, and this old grievance was cleared up. But they failed to solve the problem of Palestine. Unfortunately, at the time, the United States and Russia together, in almost identical words pressurized the British out of Palestine. Fighting began, and has continued as you know until today.

It's interesting to notice that when this plan of independent Arabs, supported by the West, keeping out other powers proved to be impracticable, Mr. Dulles and the British had another crack and they worked up a thing called the Baghdad Pact, consisting of Turkey, Persia, Iraq, and Pakistan. This is the same old principle again—support the local governments so that they'll keep the Germans and the Russians out.

Now we can get on to the events of the last summer. My own opinion, which I may as well start off with, is that the Russians laid the whole party on. I think many people when I say that are inclined to giggle, but when you've followed the whole history of the Middle East, the fact that the Russians have tried to get to the Mediterranean and to the Middle East since Catherine the Great—200 years they've been trying to do this—and the fact that every great power which has dominated Europe has started as early as possible by seizing Egypt, I think one gets a new slant on these developments. However, in actual fact it seems to me that the details of events lead to the same conclusion.

When the Egyptian army crossed the Suez Canal, it was a complete surprise to the whole world. Even the other Arab countries had no idea this was going to happen. But almost immediately the Russians issued a statement in support and said that their ships were coming through the Bosphorus. This may not be complete proof in itself, but it seems rather significant that the Russians seemed to know what Egypt was going to do before anybody else in the world. In his so-called resignation speech, President Nasser said that the Russians had told him that Israel was going to attack Syria and this had started it off. Well, you put it that way if you like, but even so you find it was the Russians who made the first move.

Now as you all remember, last June, all the press in Britain and in America went off in wild delirium of joy, saying, "Israel is our friend and she has won—Nasser was our enemy and a friend of Russia and he's lost, and therefore the Russians have taken a frightful knock in the eye." Well, the theory I wish to submit to you is that it was essential for the Russians that Egypt should be defeated.

Fortunately, ten years ago I published a book in which I wrote, "If there should ever again be fighting between Israel and Egypt, it couldn't last more than five or six days." To tell you the truth I'd forgotten all about it until somebody wrote to me last June and said, "See page so and so of your book." But I'm not telling you this to show

34

how clever I am. I'm telling you this to prove that even the most stupid people knew that this would happen. And it's quite impossible for you to convince me that the Russians thought that Egypt could defeat Israel. Therefore, the Russians knew that Egypt was going to be defeated and they wanted it that way. You may say, "But why on earth should one want one's ally to be defeated?" I think this is fairly simple also, if you assume that the Russians, as I have said, for two hundred years had been trying to pull this one off. But they couldn't, as the British and French unfortunately did, crash in like a bull in a china shop and try and take the place, because the Russians spend all their time denouncing *American* imperialism. Therefore, it was necessary to get in by some other way. But this was a very good moment because the United States was so preoccupied in Vietnam.

And so, according to my theory—you can contradict it if you like—I'm trying to justify it by logic—according to my theory the Russian plan had two stages. Stage one was to develop a threat against Israel, which was achieved by the Egyptian army crossing the Canal. The Russians knew that as soon as this happened, the United States and possibly Britain would come out with a statement in support of Israel. This was absolutely essential to the success of the Russian plan, because by that means all the Arab countries were automatically cut off from cooperation or aid from America. The next stage was to get the Arabs defeated. Then the Arabs would have to look around for somebody for help, and by a curious coincidence the Russian Ambassador was standing right there. And that, in fact, is exactly what happened. People say to me, "The Russians aren't all that cute." Well, it doesn't really make any difference—say they did it by mistake! But that is the result which they achieved.

Once again I think a mistake we make is, we say now the Israelis are extremely strong, they completely dominate the military situation, and, thank heaven, they are friends of ours. The Arabs are very weak and therefore they're no good and they are Russia's friends. But the whole point of this is not the people who live in this country but that the Arabs live along the eastern and southern shores of the Mediterranean. The lesson I have tried to draw from history is whoever holds the eastern and southern shores of the Mediterranean dominates Europe. Of course, the Arabs are not in a position to dominate Europe, and, therefore, the thing to be feared is that the Russians will hold the eastern and southern shores of the Mediterranean.

In any case whether the Russians did it on purpose or by mistake, the result is fairly sensational. As I said, for 200 years they have tried to get a fleet into the Mediterranean in vain. Until three or four years ago it was very rare if ever that you saw a Russian warship in the Mediterranean. I understand they now have a fleet of between 40 and 50 ships. These are making use of the former British naval base at Alexandria. But what is more striking is that they are now taking over the naval base in Algeria. Now this is extremely alarming because I think I am right in saying—if I am not, you can contradict me in a few minutes —I think there was a treaty between France and Algeria, when the French evacuated the country, that this naval base should be used by France for the next fifteen years.

If I am right in that, that scares me even more, because it seems to show that our great General is showing the Russians in.

Now Egypt cuts off the whole trade of Europe to the East. But Algeria is just opposite Spain, France and Italy. It is in the western Mediterranean. It is only a few miles from the Straits of Gibraltar.

It seems to me, when we weigh these things up, the argument which is often made to me, "Oh, look, the Russians lost so many million pounds worth of weapons they had given to the Egyptians." . . . But what are a few million pounds in comparison with the blockade of Europe? I believe that the whole of this has been laid on by the Russians in order to get into just that position the Arabs enjoyed for 500 years, during which they caused the whole of Europe to wither away into the Dark Ages.

Now, although the Arabs now only go as far as the border of Persia, the countries they conquered in their great time are still all Muslim, and these go on through

Persia, and up to 20 million Muslims actually in southern Soviet territory, not to mention Pakistan and detachments in Malaya, Indonesia, China, etc.

And you will remember that Mr. Dulles' Baghdad Pact selected Turkey, Persia and Pakistan as the bulwark which was to keep the Russians out. As you probably have noticed, six weeks ago, the President of Pakistan paid a state visit to Moscow.

During the course of this trip of mine, when I have been going around the United States, on two occasions, after speaking, I have been accosted by Indians who have said to me, "How wonderful to hear you put this. Everybody back home is so furious with the Americans and the British, and they think the Russians are so wonderful. It is very nice to hear an Englishman, say, take another point of view." Both these people are Hindus, not Muslims.

I have a friend who was an officer in the Arab Legion when I was there; and he is now in Malaya where he is planting tea, coffee, rubber or whatever you plant in Malaya, I am not quite sure. And he wrote to me the other day and said, "It's very unpleasant here, everybody hates the British and the Americans; they are all so angry about what's happened in the Middle East."

And so, in a word, I believe this is a plot which threatens to destroy NATO. In the course of the last month or six weeks, the President—and Mr. Dean Rusk, I think—have both made speeches or statements in which they said the North Atlantic Treaty is the basis of American policy. In other words, western Europe are the United States' best allies, and, I believe, the Russians are moving in. If they get away with it indefinitely, one by one the states of western Europe, as the Arabs are obliged to do now, will fly off to Moscow and make their own terms. Europe cannot survive if a great power holds the Middle East and North Africa.

At the same time, just at this minute, I believe that there is a moment of reaction. I believe that the Russians lead Nasser up the garden path. He didn't realize quite what he was in for, but now Egypt is suddenly realizing that she has become a Russian colony, and she is anxious to re-establish contact with the West so as not to be solely at the mercy of one great power.

There are two or three Arab states which are very difficult, notably Syria and now, unfortunately, Algeria, but people always quote what Nasser or Egypt has said and say, "The Arabs say this or the Arabs say that." I would like to draw your attention to the fact that there are thirteen Arab states in the United Nations, and I reckon that nine of those are still firmly based on the Western Powers. And so my immediate plea is this. I do not for one moment suggest that the United States should now abandon Israel or arm the Arabs against her. However, I do think you might exercise a little attempt to control her because every step forward the Israelis make from now onward, more Arabs will say to the Russians, for heaven's sake come here. Israel completely dominates the military situation, and there is no use mincing matters about it.

Secondly, if you cannot make friends at once with Syria or Algeria, we will say, why not let's show ourselves a bit friendly with some of the nine other ones? The majority of these have not been in the least involved in the operations of this summer. You can start and count them up from Lebanon, Iraq is a bit doubtful perhaps, but I think is win-backable if that is the correct word, Kuwait, Saudi Arabia, Sudan, Libya, Tunisia, Morocco—I think I have forgotten a couple somewhere. Anyhow, there are more Arab states that are still based on the West than there are which are entirely in the hands of Russia.

Personally, I should like to see the really great powers intervene and say this is the answer to your dispute and what's more you've all got to behave yourselves and we guarantee everybody's frontiers. We could have done this—in fact, to some extent we did in 1948 when the United States, Britain and France guaranteed the borders after the first burst of fighting.

Now we can no longer do it because the Russians are there and so if we are going to have a stabilizing guarantee you've got to have Russia in with the United States. This might or might not be possible, I don't know. It seems to me the best thing if it can be done. But if

38

it can't be done, if the Russians won't cooperate, if they can see their profit in further trouble, for heaven's sake, my plea is don't let's lump all the Arabs together. Let's make friends with the nine, some of whom are thousands of miles from the scene of this conflict. And if the Russians do get well dug in, in two or three Arab countries, well then the Western Powers will be dug in in the intervening Arab countries, and we shall have a sort of chess board with the alternative countries, some on the eastern side and some on the west.

But I feel most strongly that if the United States stands out now and remains aloof, all the Arab countries will give up hope; they will all believe that Britain and America are solely favorable to Israel, and they will all fly off to Russia, and that means the virtual withering up of the wealth of Europe, the collapse of the North Atlantic Treaty, and the United States' remaining without allies.

Arnold Joseph Toynbee, a British historian, received his D. Litt. at Oxford. He was a member of the Middle Eastern section of the British delegation to the Peace Conference in Paris (1919). Long a professor of Byzantine and Modern Greek language, literature and history at the University of London, and now Professor Emeritus, Dr. Tyonbee is the author of many scholarly works, among them "A Study of History" (12 volumes). He is an editor of several publications, including "British Commonwealth Relations," and "Survey of International Affairs."

Reprinted from "Mid East," June/July, 1967.

THE MIDDLE EAST, PAST AND PRESENT
Arnold J. Toynbee

I will try to put, first, the Israelis' view of this as I see it, then the Arabs' view, and thirdly my own view. I am neither an Arab nor an Israeli. I am British, so I feel deeply my country's share in the responsibility for this tragic conflict between two other peoples. Britain issued the Balfour Declaration in 1917—Britain was in power in Palestine for 30 years ending in 1948—and Britain's precipitate abdication in Palestine after World War II left the way open in 1948 for the first of the three Arab-Israeli wars.

Israelis' Views

We are Jews, the living representatives of Judah, one of the 12 tribes of Israel that conquered most of Palestine in the 13th Century B.C. We held Judah's share of the conquered territory for seven centuries, until we were deported by Nebuchadnezzar in 587 B.C. We were back again within less than half a century, and we then held Judaea, once more, for the next 773 years, until we were evicted by the Romans in 135 A.D. We have never renounced our claim to the land of Israel. We have always hoped, believed and

41

proclaimed that we shall get this land back again. It is our land, we contend.

After another 1,883 years (continuing the Israelis' view) we did recover a foothold there in 1918, and during the half century since then, by devoted hard work, ability and military valor, we have built up our present national state of Israel, and have inflicted three smashing defeats on the Arabs, who have been trying to evict us once again.

We want to have a country of our own again, like other peoples and like our own ancestors. We also need to have a country of our own, because, since the conversion of the Roman empire to Christianity in the 4th Century A.D., we have been penalized and persecuted by the Western Christian majority among whom we have had to live. This persecution has culminated in the unprecedented crime of genocide which has been committed against us in our lifetime by a Western people, the Germans, in Europe. We are not going to let the Arabs commit the same crime of genocide against us here, in our own land of Israel.

Arabs' Views

In 1918, ninety per cent of the population of Palestine was Arab, and Palestine had been ours since we conquered it from the Romans in the 7th Century A.D. Since 1918, a militant and aggressive foreign body has been thrust into the heart of our Arab world. This has been done, against our protests, by force of arms—British force until, under the protection of British bayonets, the Zionist Jewish intruders had built up sufficient force of their own to be more than a match for our Arab strength. Then the British scuttled, and left us to our fate. Our fate had been that 900,000 Palestinian Arabs (there are more than a million of these now) have been forcibly deprived of their homes and property and have been turned into refugees, living on a dole. Any Palestinian Arab refugee who tries to return home and resume possession of his property is shot by the Israelis, who have robbed us of our country and property. The Palestinian Arabs who have not lost their homes are being treated by the Israelis, under whose rule they have

42

fallen, as penalized second-class citizens. The Arab territory that the Israelis have seized by force stretches from the Mediterranean to the Red Sea at Elath. This foreign-occupied territory cuts the Arab world in two.

The Israelis' crime against the Arabs is flagrant (the Arabs would go on to say), but it is not the Arabs who have committed crimes against the Jews. When we conquered Palestine from the Romans, we allowed Jews to reside in Judaea again for the first time in 500 years. When we conquered Spain from the German Goths, we liberated the Jews in Spain from the Goths' Nazi-like oppression of them. The Prophet Muhammad in the Qur'an had commanded Muslims to tolerate and protect law-abiding Jews and Christians under Muslim rule, and our Muslim Arab record, in acting up to this commandment, has been fine compared with the Western people's treatment of the Jews. Yet now we have been made to pay for a Western people's crime against the Jews. The Germans tried to exterminate the Jews.

The Western victors in World War II, the Americans, above all (the Arab argument goes on), have made the Arabs, not the Germans, pay for the Germans' crime. In Western eyes, the Germans may be criminals, but they are also fellow Westerners, so they are privileged. We Arabs do not count. We are "natives," just part of the fauna of Palestine. We have no human rights. The Israelis, on the other hand, have the West's ear, the West's sympathy, and the West's support. In Western countries, the Jews have money-power and voting power, which we Arabs do not have there. Also, the West, unlike us Arabs, has a bad conscience about its past treatment of the Jews. So the West wants to compensate the Jews—as long as this is done, not at the West's own expense, but at ours.

We are never going to submit to this injustice, the Arabs say. The Israeli intruders are the spearhead of Western new-imperialism in the Arab world. We have suffered from Western aggression in Palestine once before. That time, it was the Crusaders. We succeeded in expelling the Crusaders, though that took us 200 years. We are going to expel the Israelis too, however long this make take us.

By 1948, the Palestinian Arabs had been the inhabitants of Palestine for more than 1,300 years. This length of time has given them a prescriptive right to continue to live in Palestine and to retain their property there. As for the Jews' claim to have a right to reoccupy Palestine, the statute of limitations applies to this. The Israelis have no right to keep the Palestinian Arabs out of their homes and to rob them of their property, as they have done.

A distinction has to be drawn between two different claims put forward by the Jews. Their claim against the Germans for reparation (so far as any kind of reparation can be made for mass murder) is 100 per cent justified. It is not at all unreasonable for the Jews to claim that their cumulative experience of criminal treatment by Westerners entitled them to have a country of their own. But then they should have been given German territory (e.g., the Rhine-land), not Arab territory, as the site for a Jewish state. And also, from the beginning of the persecution of the Jews in Germany, Britain and the United States could, and should, have given all the Jewish refugees asylum in their own territories. They should not have laid on Palestine any part of a burden that was bound to strain still further already strained relations between Jews and Arabs there.

The Jews' claim to recover possession of Palestine after 1,883 years is different in kind from their claim against Germany, and is not of equal validity. This historical claim was justifiable insofar—but only insofar—as it is compatible with the rights of the Palestinian Arabs. The Jews do have a right of free access to the territory, in Palestine, of the ancient kingdom of Judah, which they held for two periods in the now rather distant past. They have an unquestionable right to reside in Judaea for religious purposes. Subject to the consent of the Arab inhabitants, they also had a right to buy land in Palestine from Arab owners, and to plant Jewish settlers on purchased land in numbers that would not have threatened to swamp the Arab population. But they have had no right to seize by military force the terri-tory that has now become the state of Israel, and to turn its Arab inhabitants into either second-class citizens of

44

Israel or into refugees whom the Israelis are depriving of their homes and their property.

The existence and presence of the state of Israel and of the Israeli people are now facts, and it has been demonstrated that these facts cannot be undone. Moreover, if they could have been undone, the effect would have been to create a new horde of refugees—Israeli refugees this time. Yet, if you or I were Arabs, we should surely feel about Israel as the Arabs feel.

One of the two main obstacles to a solution of the Arab-Israeli conflict is the Arabs' unwillingness, so far, to accept the hard fact that the establishment of the state of Israel, within the limits set by the armistice lines agreed on in 1948, is an accomplished fact which the Arabs, too, have to recognize and accept. The other obstacle is the present plight of the Palestinian Arabs. These two obstacles are interrelated, and unless and until both obstacles are overcome, the conflict will continue.

The Guilt of the West

The parties who are principally responsible for this conflict are neither the Israelis nor the Arabs themselves. They are three Western peoples: the British, the Germans, the Americans. We Westerners have a major responsibility for opening the way for a reconciliation between the Israelis and the Arabs by finding ways and means of doing justice to the Palestinian Arabs—justice that will be felt to be adequate by the refugees and by the Arab world as a whole, and, at the same time, will not be a threat, as the unsolved Arab refugee problem has been so far, to Israel's security and, indeed, existence.

After the third Arab-Israeli war, it is imperative that there should be not just a renewal of the previous truce but a permanent peace settlement between Israel and the Arab states. To be permanent, this peace settlement must not be imposed by force. It must be one that is accepted by both belligerents, not just on paper, but in their hearts. Only a peace settlement that is recognized by both sides to have been genuinely accepted by both sides can open the way for reconciliation and cooperation between them.

The tests of Israel's sincerity will be that she makes it quite clear that she is making no territorial claims beyond the 1948 armistice lines (which, of course, implies withdrawing from all territory beyond these lines occupied in June 1967) and also that she cooperates actively in the indemnification and permanent resettlement of the Palestinian Arab refugees. Every one of these refugees who is offered, and who accepts, repatriation inside Israel's borders will be a help towards turning enmity into friendship. The tests of the Arab states' sincerity will be that they, on their side, cooperate actively in the permanent resettlement of the refugees, and that they cease to use the refugees either as political pawns or as potential infiltrators, encamped around Israel's borders. From the humanitarian point of view, permanent resettlement is, of course, in the best interests of the refugees themselves.

The Danger of War

The whole human race is an interested party, because, so long as the Arab-Israeli conflict continues, it may at any moment produce a clash between the United States and the Soviet Union, and this might lead to an atomic third world war. The world simply cannot afford to acquiesce in the continuance of this explosive local situation.

In working for reconciliation, our primary concern should be with the welfare of individual human beings, Arab and Israeli human beings alike, not with the power or prestige of states, small or great. The basic principle for a settlement should be: "The minimum possible amount of human suffering for all human beings concerned—Arabs, Israelis and the rest of mankind."

Since 1948 there has been in impasse. The Palestinian Arab refugees and the Arab states have been declaring their intentions of getting rid of the Israeli foreign body that has been thrust into the Arab world by force at the Arabs' expense. This Arab refusal to accept the establishment of Israel as a permanently accomplished fact has been only human. But it has also been only human that the Israelis, on their side, should be unwilling, so long as the Arabs maintain this stand, to consider taking any steps towards

46

righting the wrongs that they have done to the Palestinian Arabs insofar as these steps might involve readmitting Arab refugees into Israeli territory—and, so long as the Palestinian refugees' wrongs remain unredressed, the Arabs will remain determined to expel the Israelis, as they previously expelled the Crusaders. Here is the vicious circle that we have to break.

Making Concessions

This vicious circle can be broken, because there are the makings of a settlement based on reciprocal concessions by the Arabs and the Israelis, the combined effect of which would be in the common interest of the two parties—and of the world. These reciprocal concessions will have to be made simultaneously. The Arabs will have to declare—and this sincerely, really meaning what they say—that they now recognize that the state of Israel has come to stay, and that they now renounce their previous intention to destroy it, subject to the condition that justice will now be done to the Palestinian Arabs. Simultaneously, the Israelis will have to admit that they have done the Palestinian Arabs a great injury, and to declare—they, too, meaning what they say—that they will now do justice to the Palestinian Arabs, subject to the existence of Israel now being recognized genuinely, as a permanent fact, by the Palestinian Arabs themselves and by the Arab states.

Obviously the key to a general reconciliation lies in reconciling the Arabs, especially the refugees outside Israel, but also the Arabs still inside Israel as well, to the existence of Israel in their midst.

If Israel were assured that the Arabs inside Israel were not going to be used as a "fifth column" against her, she could afford to treat them as first-class citizens. If she were assured that any of the refugees that she readmitted could not be used as a "fifth column" either, she could afford to readmit some, at any rate, of the refugees. To be assured of this Israel must be convinced of the genuineness of the indispensable Arab undertaking to accept the existence of Israel and no longer to seek to destroy her.

Reinstate the Refugees

It is important to readmit into Isreal, on this condition, as many of the Arab refugees as possible, and to reinstate them, as far as possible, in their own homes and property, or, alternatively, to give them new homes and property of equal value inside Israel. If the hitherto unsurmounted political obstacle could be cleared out of the way, modern technology could provide a livelihood, within the borders of Israel, not only for the whole present population, both Israeli and Arab, but for the Arab refugees too. We are on the verge of succeeding in desalinating sea-water at an economic price, and this is going to transform deserts into fertile fields.

The ideal solution would be to repatriate all the refugees. This would be the surest road to a reconciliation, because Palestine is a country that keeps its hold on the heartstrings of any people that has ever lived there. The Jews' longing to return to Palestine has never died since their first expulsion in 587 B.C. The Arab Palestinian refugees have the same feelings today. When I talked to them in the Gaza Strip, I could have fancied that I was talking to the Jewish refugees of the first generation who wept when they sat down by the waters of Babylon.

However, it seems improbable that many of the present Arab refugees will wish to return to their homes now that this will mean coming under Israeli rule, even if the Israelis were to give them first-class citizen treatment. It also seems improbable that the Israelis would be willing to readmit all the Arab refugees, even if they were convinced that these would not try to act as a "fifth column." Therefore many, perhaps a majority, of the Palestinian Arab refugees will have to be resettled somewhere else. Can they be reconciled to this second-best alternative? This depends on whether good enough permanent homes can be found for them, and good enough new opportunities can be opened up for them, in place of the present refugee camps in the Gaza Strip, which is congested with refugee camps and is anyway a poor country in which the refugees have poor prospects.

Success also depends on whether the money can be found, not only for compensating the refugees adequately for their property in Israel, but for resettling them comfortably and for giving them first-rate educational facilities. The refugees also have a right to a handsome bonus in compensation for their having been left to languish as refugees for 20 years. (The blame for this act of inhumanity falls not only on the Israelis, but also on the Arab states, which have, unlike the West Germans, been unwilling to give hospitality, even temporarily, to refugees who are their kith and kin, but have used them, cynically, as political pawns. It must be added, however, that the refugees themselves, so far, have been unwilling to accept any alternative to repatriation in their Palestinian homes, and this not under Israeli rule. This stand taken by the refugees has been natural, though it has been unrealistic.)

There would be no difficulty about finding the money. The whole world would be eager to pay through the nose for the sake of getting rid of a conflict which threatens to precipitate an atomic third world war. Large funds will be needed for both resettlement and for education.

A possible region for rehousing Palestinian Arab refugees who wish to preserve their corporate identity as a community would be the part of Syria lying to the northeast of the Euphrates River. This fertile territory is, so far, only sparsely populated. Much of it is cultivated by rainwater—and Syria and Iraq have been getting together for building a barrage on the Euphrates that would not only prevent flooding but would also provide water for irrigation.

It is equally important that the Palestinian Arab refugees should be provided with first-rate facilities for education. Those few of them who have succeeded already in getting higher education under their present adverse conditions have demonstrated that the Palestinian Arabs are an intellectually able people, like the Lebanese, Armenians, Jews and Parsees. All the countries of the world can contribute to the healing of the Arab-Israeli conflict by opening their doors wide to Palestinian Arabs of proven ability. We would all admit them to our universities, allow them to find employment in our respective countries, and also allow them to become naturalized citizens of our countries if they have made good among us and if they wish to become permanent members

49

of our respective communities. They would make valuable new citizens—especially for countries that still need new citizens, such as Brazil, Venezuela, Australia, Canada and, above all, the United States.

Be Magnanimous

Psychologically, it is important that Israel, when once the Arabs have genuinely made peace with her, should take the initiative in proposing plans on the lines sketched above and in raising the necessary funds. The hour of military victory is the moment for being magnanimous and far-sighted. The party whose military weakness has just been exposed for the third time is the party that will be particularly bitter and sensitive. If a settlement based solidly on reciprocal concessions is to be reached, the concessions that the Arabs will have to make will be much more painful than what will be required of the Israelis.

A genuine permanent reconciliation with the Arabs is a vital interest of Israel's. It is vital for her because even the most sensational military victories are wasting assets. I would therefore beg the Israelis to recall something that was said by the founder and first rector of the Hebrew University of Jerusalem, the late Dr. Judah Leon Magnes, a distinguished Jewish American who did so much for re-creating a Jewish national home in Palestine. Dr. Magnes, who died in 1948, said repeatedly that the only sure permanent basis for the renewed presence of a Jewish community in Palestine was Arab goodwill. The Jews, Dr. Magnes held, could not retain their renewed foothold in Palestine permanently just by military force. This is as true today as it was when Dr. Magnes first said it.

At the present moment, the Israelis are naturally elated. Being human, they might be tempted to be presumptuous and arrogant. This is the moment at which they should give ear to the voice of their wise and noble-minded compatriot, Dr. Magnes.

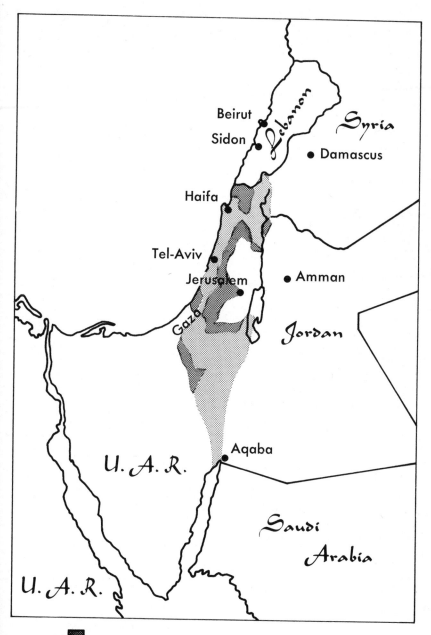

Beirut

Sidon

Lebanon

Syria

● Damascus

Haifa

Tel-Aviv

Jerusalem

Gaza

● Amman

Jordan

Aqaba

U. A. R.

Saudi Arabia

U. A. R.

Areas held by Israel after the Armistice, 1949.

The Rt. Hon. Anthony Nutting, P.C., was Parliamentary Under-Secretary of State for Foreign Affairs, 1951-1954, and Minister of State at the Foreign Office from 1954 until his resignation in 1956. While Minister of State, he led the U.K. delegation to the U.N. General Assembly and to the U.N. Disarmament Commission. His most recent books are "Lawrence of Arabia" (1961), "The Arabs" (1964), "Gordon of Khartoum" (1966) and "No End of a Lesson" (1967).

This article was originally delivered at the Leon Lowenstein Auditorium of the Congregation Emanu-El, New York City, as a public address preceding the 23rd Annual Conference of the American Council for Judaism in New York City on November 2, 1967.

Palestine which followed the Balfour Declaration and the establishment of the British mandate, because if we are to understand—still more to resolve—the current political crisis arising out of the Arab-Israeli war of last June, it is essential that we should recall just how this present impasse was reached.

First, we cannot forget—for if we forget no Arab will forget—that in 1915 Great Britain promised to Sharif Hussein of Mecca that in return for the help of his Arab armies in the campaign against Turkey, Germany's ally in World War I, all Palestine plus Iraq, Syria and Transjordan and the Arabian Peninsula would be free and independent once their Turkish rulers had been defeated. No sooner had this pledge been given and the Arab armies mobilized in response, in the common allied cause, than Great Britain and France got together and, in the infamous Sykes-Picot agreement of 1916, agreed to parcel out Syria, Iraq and Transjordan between them as the spoils of war. Following upon this, to complete the double-cross, in November 1917, exactly 50 years ago today, Great Britain decided to take over Palestine as a strategic base from which to defend the Suez Canal under the humanitarian umbrella of the Balfour Declaration.

Small wonder that the Arabs felt betrayed by this cynical breach of the solemn pledges of independence which had been given to Sharif Hussein and to the Arab peoples. But still, because of a touching faith in their erstwhile allies, they allowed themselves to be mollified by a further series of pledges and assurances. The national home, they were assured, would not be allowed to become a national state and the civil and religious rights of the non-Jewish communities—which, to say the least, was a quaint, if not a rather sinister, description of an overwhelming Arab majority —would be safeguarded. Therefore, the Arabs felt that perhaps, after all, the denial of the pledges of independence might only be temporary. When all was said and done the Arabs of Palestine did then number 92% of the population and the Jews, only 8%. And so, armed with these assurances, such Arab leaders as the Emir Faisal agreed to cooperate in the creation of a refuge for the Jewish people in Palestine from the persecutions of Europe.

After all, such cooperation was in full and total harmony with the traditional hospitality which the Arabs had extended down the centuries to the persecuted Jews of Europe, from the Spanish Inquisition right through to the pogroms of Czarist Russia. The one people, the only people, in the whole so-called civilized world who had never persecuted Jews were the Arabs. In Palestine, even as late as 1948, so close was the relationship between Jew and Arab that each and every child born in the same week, whether Jewish or Arab, became automatically a foster brother and foster sister of the other. Ladies and gentlemen, I defy anybody to find a closer human relationship between two segments of the same race. Even the Grand Mufti of Jerusalem himself, who led the Arab rebellion from 1936 to 1939 against the Zionist agents in Palestine, even the arch-enemy of Jewish settlement, Haj Amin al-Husseini, had three Jewish foster brothers.

Thus, provided that the rights of the Arabs were not threatened, in all the circumstances and with all the history of Arab-Jewish cooperation, it seemed both natural and right, as the Emir Faisal had agreed with Dr. Chaim Weizmann in 1919, that "all necessary measures shall be taken to encourage Jewish immigration on a large scale and to settle Jewish immigrants upon the land." Alas, poor Faisal and his fellow Arab leaders, both inside and outside Palestine, did not reckon with the determination of the Zionist Movement to create, not a home, but a state and a state which, in the words of Dr. Weizmann, would be "as Jewish as Britain is British." Nor did Emir Faisal reckon with the weakness of successive British governments in the face of this determined Zionist pressure, a weakness which allowed the Jewish Agency to be established and to become a government within the Mandatory government of Palestine, while the Arabs were denied any effective say in the administration of their country whatsoever, a weakness which permitted the Zionist Agency to buy at knock-down prices land owned by Syrian and Lebanese landowners who were cut off from their properties by the international frontiers separating British from French mandated territories. That weakness also permitted the Zionist Agency to evict thousands of Arab tenant and farm workers to make way for Jewish settlers from Europe, compensating these tenants and workers at times with as little as ten dollars per family.

After nearly ten years of this treatment, Britain in 1930 at long last appeared to recognize the need to protect the rights of the Arabs by a closer control of Jewish immigration and by protection for the Arab peasants and tenant farmers. But it only required the threat of Dr. Weizmann to resign the presidency of the World Zionist Organization to force Mr. Ramsay MacDonald, the British Prime Minister, to reverse his position and to revert to the policy of giving the Zionists a free hand in Palestine. Soon after this the rise of Hitler in Nazi Germany created a steep rise in Jewish immigration. The Jewish proportion of the population climbed from 8% to 30%. The Arabs protested that they were being squeezed out. And again for a brief moment the British government recognized their claims and offered a legislative assembly, to be elected by proportional representation, which would give the Arabs a majority vote—not much after the other Arab mandated territories under Britain, Iraq, Transjordan and Egypt, had become completely independent. But once again the British government was forced to back down in face of protests from the Zionists, who feared that a legislative assembly with an Arab majority would threaten their plans to create a national Jewish state in Palestine.

The Arabs, now driven to desperation, decided that armed rebellion was the only way to assert their rights. From 1936 to 1939 the rebellion continued, led by the Grand Mufti of Jerusalem. The Arabs lost far more heavily in human lives and treasure than either the Jews or the British, but still they carried on the struggle. By 1939 the British government was finally driven to accept the fact that the Arabs had a case and that something must be done to make amends for the shameful way in which they had been betrayed and their rights had been ignored. A conference was called in London of all parties to the Palestine dispute and when, inevitably, no agreement was reached, the British government decided to impose a solution, the famous White Paper solution of 1939. Palestine, it was decided, after an interval of ten years was to be an independent, bi-national state with Arabs and Jews sharing in the government and insuring the essential interests of both communities. Immigration was to continue for five years at a predetermined rate of 15,000 a year after which any further immigration was to be by agreement with the Arabs. And the Arabs were to be protected against land purchase and land acquisition by the Zionist Agency.

This was by far the best, the wisest and the fairest solution yet contrived and had World War II not broken out a few months later it might have resolved the problem. But with Germany at her throat, Great Britain was no longer in a position to impose any solution on Palestine and by the end of the war Britain was too exhausted to cope any longer. The unspeakable atrocities of the gas chambers of Nazi Germany and of the occupied territories of Europe had turned the flow of Jewish migrants into Palestine into a flood totally beyond the capacity of Great Britain to control. In desperation, the British government handed its Mandate over Palestine back to the League of Nation's successor, the United Nations, to do their worst. Which is precisely what they did, by partitioning Palestine into six areas, three for the Jews and three for the Arabs— and incidentally, in the manner which gave to the Jewish areas all the best of the land and left the Arabs with the wilderness of Judea and the hills of northern Galilee.

Now from this moment when the United Nations passed this partition resolution, in November, 1947, until the departure of the British forces from Palestine in May 1943, when the Israeli state was formally established, the Zionists, aided by the Stern gang, went to work; went to work to persuade the Arabs to leave the areas which were to form the Israeli state. To reinforce the argument that such Arabs would have no place in Israel, the Stern gang, as some of you will remember, selected a few villages such as Deir Yassin to stage a massacre of the Arab inhabitants to create a general state of panic and hence an exodus of the Arab population. So that by May 1948, when Britain formally and finally abandoned her responsibility for Palestine, more than 300,000 Arabs had been evicted from their homes and farms and had become the first installment of that hapless, hopeless, homeless group of suffering humanity known today as the Palestine refugees.

Zionist propaganda would have us believe that the Palestine refugees are the product of the Arab attack on Israel in 1948 and that they were ordered to flee from their homes by their own Arab leaders, who promised that they would be restored when the Arabs had liquidated the state of Israel. The truth is the exact opposite. Before the Arabs attacked in May 1948, the Arab refugees numbered over 300,000; they had been ordered—nay forced—to leave by the Zionists who had neither use nor room for them in the areas of Palestine alloted to the Israeli state. Thus it would be truer to say that the refugees were the cause of the first Arab-Israeli war and not the result.

Of course, when the Arabs subsequently lost the war, in 1949, the first war, and lost northern Galilee and much of the territory alloted to them under the partition plan, the number of refugees increased considerably; doubled in fact, by the exodus from the areas newly conquered by the Israeli army. But just as, last June, it did not require exhortation from their leaders—indeed last June, if you remember, the Arabs left the west bank of Jordan against the exhortation of their leaders who told them to stay, and yet 175,000 still left—just like last June, it did not require exhortation from their leaders to make them leave in 1948 and 1949. The Arabs left because they panicked, as civil populations do panic in war, as the army of the conquering hordes spreads across their land, as the French and the Belgians and the Dutch panicked in 1940; or because they were evicted to make way for Israeli settlement of the conquered territories. Suffice it to say that when the dust of battle had cleared, the Arabs were worse off than ever in terms of territory and nearly 700,000 of their fellows from the Israeli occupied areas found themselves thrown on the charity of the Arab states and the United Nations for a bare subsistence and denied the opportunity to return to lands which they and their ancestors had owned and worked for thirteen centuries of human history.

And as the humiliation at their defeat and at the injustice done to the Arabs of Palestine rose in the throats

58

of all the Arab world, they cast about for an explanation: How had this come upon them? Britain, they reckoned, had taken Palestine in the first place, in violation of her pledges to the Arabs, for imperialist and strategic reasons to establish a base from which to exercise a dominant influence in and around the Arab world. There was too much truth in this theory for it to be easily dismissed. World War II, they reckoned, had exhausted Britain's resources and she was no longer able to sustain such a base for herself. So, she and her Western allies had introduced this alien, Western, European state of Israel to do for her and for them what she could no longer do for herself: to take over the garrison role which Britain no longer had the capacity to sustain; to act as a beachhead for British and Western purposes and designs upon the Arab world. These dark suspicions were tragically confirmed at Suez in 1956 when Britain and France, using Israel as their stalking-horse, invaded Egypt in a desperate attempt to seize control of the Suez Canal.

So much for the background to this tragic conflict between the Arabs and Israel. The rest is too well known for me to need to repeat it tonight: the refusal of the Arab states to recognize the state of Israel and the refusal of Israel to repatriate the Palestine refugees; the continuation of the state of war and the denial of passage for Israeli ships through the Suez Canal and the Gulf of Aqaba and the long stalemate broken by the Suez episode in 1956, which we might call round two, and punctuated by raids and reprisals across Israel's borders—a long stalemate which lasted until June of this year.

What we have to do now, and what I ask you to do now with me, is to address ourselves to the present day and to examine what, if anything, can be done to bring about a just and honorable settlement.

To put it bluntly, we have a situation today in which Israel, after the third round in the bitter running conflict with the Arabs, bestrides not just the U.N. partition frontiers nor just the frontiers which she gained by conquest in 1949, but the whole of the former state of Palestine, including the old city of Jerusalem, the third holy city in the

59

Muslim world, together, for good measure, with the Sinai Peninsula. And Israel, it appears, is determined to stay in these areas, even to introduce Jewish settlements into them, while, for her own part, she still refuses to acknowledge any debt to the Palestine refugees who paid the price and are still paying the price for what Europe did to the Jewish people—paying the debt which Europe owes to the persecuted Jews of the world. Israel has made great play with the refusal in the past years of the Arabs to recognize her existence. Likewise, she has claimed that the continued state of belligerency on the part of the Arabs constitutes a permanent threat to her existence. And she has complained bitterly about the refusal of the Arabs to allow her freedom of navigation through the Suez Canal and the Gulf of Aqaba. The last of these, the Gulf of Aqaba, as you remember, was the immediate cause of the outbreak of the war in June of this year.

But now the Arabs are prepared to concede all these demands, as has been evidenced by their endorsement of the Indian and Latin American resolutions before the United Nations Security Council. The Arabs will recognize more than that. They will respect the territorial integrity and political independence of the state of Israel. That is in the resolution. The Arabs will terminate the state of belligerency. That is in the resolution. And they will guarantee freedom of navigation through the international waterways in the area. That, too, is in the resolution if, in return, Israel will withdraw from the Arab territory which she seized last June and will contribute to a just settlement of the Arab refugees.

Surely no impartial observer could find fault with such terms. Yet it seems that this is not enough for the state of Israel. From the latest utterances of Premier Eshkol it seems that, having pocketed these far-reaching and fundamental concessions from the Arabs which could give Israel all the security and peace that she seeks, Israel is not prepared to withdraw, still less to settle the Palestine refugees in their own homeland, and now demands individual negotiations with each individual, separate Arab state, and negotiations under the duress of Israeli occupation of that

60

state's territory. Ladies and gentlemen, this is the doctrine of "divide and conquer" and these are conquerors' terms. If Israel persists in these terms, there will be no peace in the Middle East. Counsels of moderation such as Abdel Nasser was able to impose upon his colleagues in the recent Khartoum summit conference of Arab states will be rejected. The doves will have lost out and the hawks will say "we told you so." And I don't have to tell you who the Arab hawks will be. And the conflict will continue between the Arab states and Israel until a fourth or a fifth or a sixth round finally plunges the whole Middle East into a holocaust, when one or possibly both sides dispose of the nuclear weapon.

There is a dangerous tendency among many Arabs to equate the present situation with that of the Crusades. "It took us," I've heard this often said by Arabs, "It took us 200 years to get rid of the Crusaders. All right! If Israel will make no terms, if Israel will make no amends to the Palestine people, we will wait 200 years and we will get rid of them in the end as we got rid of the Crusaders, another alien state, another European incursion, another western beachhead upon our shores. We will get rid of it."

This is dangerous talk because Saladin, who finally destroyed the Crusader state, fought Richard Coeur-de-Lion with swords and lances and not with atomic bombs, and yet this is the prospect for the Middle East in the fourth or the fifth or the sixth or some round, if nothing is done to bring a just and honorable settlement today.

Meanwhile the relative calm on the West Bank of today which we hear about from the Zionists—how happy the Arabs are to be selling postcards to all those nice tourists from Israel—this relative calm, ladies and gentlemen, is largely due to the state of shock of the inhabitants, and it will give way, all too soon, if nothing is done, to a state of guerrilla war in which the Israelis will be driven to use ever more brutal methods of suppression, just as the Germans and the Japanese and the Italians were forced to escalate their suppression of national resistance movements in occupied territories in World War II. I was in France in 1940 and I remember exactly the same feeling, the same atmosphere amongst the French people as I am told now exists on the West Bank of the Jordan. How pleased the French were to be out of the war! How thankful they were that the Germans, far from being terrible people, behaved so correctly! No women were raped, no babies were butchered. And yet, ladies and gentlemen, not many months afterwards, somebody lost his head and somebody else lost his temper and somebody started shooting and the Germans shot back. And by 1944, innocent men and women were being taken out and shot as hostages because somebody had blown a bridge five miles away.

I don't care who the occupying power is. These are the sort of bestialities to which occupation gets driven by national resistance movements such as will come on the West Bank of the Jordan, and in the Gaza Strip, so long as Israel struts and strides in those areas, insisting upon conqueror's terms. And it is surely inconceivable that sane men in Israel or anywhere else, however callous they may be to the sufferings of humanity, it is surely inconceivable that sane men could invite such a prospect upon themselves. It is surely inconceivable that the United Nations could permit such a disaster to be perpetrated. Yet if nothing is done, and if nothing is done now; if the United Nations fails to endorse the terms and the concessions offered by the Arab states for a settlement: recognition, termination of the state of belligerency and freedom of passage for Israeli shipping through Suez and Aqaba; and if Israel cannot be induced to accept and to honor these terms and to do, for her part, what is necessary to bring about a settlement—then, ladies and gentlemen, these disasters will happen as surely as we are sitting in this hall tonight, however much it may cost the Arab world.

There is an old Arab couplet by an unknown poet which demonstrates my argument far more eloquently than I could.

Let none be with us proud or overbearing,
For we can be more foolish and more daring.

And however foolish or foolhardy it may seem to some people, the Arabs will never abandon the cause of their dispossessed brothers of Palestine and will never accept that

62

the land of Palestine shall remain as it is today under the occupation of an alien Western state. Everything else, everything else—Aqaba, Suez, frontiers, Syrian Heights, Gaza Strip, even the city of Jerusalem—everything else is comparatively a side issue relative to this basic human issue of the people of Palestine. This is what this conflict is all about and this is the issue that has to be settled.

You and I know, ladies and gentlemen, that there is only one nation in the world today which can induce the Israelis to settle it, to accept the terms now offered by the Arabs, and to redress the wrongs done to the people of Palestine. There is only one nation that can do this and that is the United States of America. In 1956, when Israel had conquered far less territory than today, after the Suez episode, the United States told her to withdraw. Britain and France objected; they had to: they had gone into the thing with Israel. They said "These people are misunderstood, they've suffered a terrible injustice, they should not be asked to withdraw unconditionally." But the United States said, "Withdraw!" and so the Israelis withdrew. Today no such American pressures seem to be available and Israel is able, indeed encouraged, by this totally negative attitude in Washington to stand pat upon her conquests. And once again to the Arabs the Western world seems to be encouraging Israel to expand at the expense of the Arabs. Once again the suspicions of the Arabs are confirmed that Israel was created and is still being used as a Western outpost to dominate an Eastern race.

Through you therefore, ladies and gentlemen, tonight I would issue this appeal on this historic occasion, the fiftieth anniversary of the Balfour Declaration. I would issue this appeal through you to the government of the United States. In the name of everything that you want to see created in the Middle East, stability, security and peace for all nations in the area, and in the interests of America's best relations with the Arab and the Muslim world, use your influence on Israel to accept an honorable and just peace such as is now within her grasp, such as the Arabs have now offered, and to work out through the United Nations the means by which such terms can be translated into effect.

Perhaps I might be permitted to add this further thought as to what sort of settlement might emerge for the future and I hope I shall not be thought too starry-eyed an idealist in what I have to propose. I think I've said enough of the dangers and the disasters that are implicit in the present stalemate. There is, however, one aspect of the situation, of this highly explosive and dangerous situation in the Middle East today, which might be turned to the account of a truly imaginative solution.

I have always felt, and many people who knew Palestine in the old days agree with me on this that, quite apart from the human problems that are involved, the human suffering of the people of Palestine, one of the worst results of creating a Western Zionist state in the Middle East was that, in doing so, we destroyed the state of Palestine by carving it into two or rather into six different parts. For the state of Palestine, notwithstanding all that happened in the 1920's and the 1930's, was by far the most cultured and educated state in the Arab world and had been so ever since the days of the Ottoman Empire. Now, it just so happens that geographically Palestine has been reunited— by conquest and occupation, yes—but reunited, nonetheless. Is it too much to hope that such counsels of wisdom and imagination might prevail even at this late hour amongst Israel's leaders as would enable the state of Palestine to be recreated not just geographically but politically as a bi-national, multi-racial state? Is it too much to ask that Israel should say openly, and mean it, that a Palestinian Arab has the same rights to live and work in Palestine as a Palestinian Jew, and to share on equal terms with his Jewish cousins in the running of his country, insuring that the essential interests of each community are safeguarded and preserved?

Now, ladies and gentlemen, before any of you dismiss this idea as the ravings of a lunatic internationalist, which perhaps I may be, let me ask you what you would have thought in World War II if I had come to you and said that the answer to the problem of Europe was for France and Germany together to create a European community in which they would pool their economic resources and work towards the creation of a European political federation. You would have said, "He is a raving lunatic internationalist." And yet, ladies and gentlemen, twelve years after the war ended this is precisely what France and Germany did, and are doing today. Twelve years after the end of World War II! And France and Germany, after all, had a tradition of mutual enmity, jealousy and hatred which has never existed, could not exist, between Arab and Jew. Is it so impossible to create a bi-national state out of what are after all two segments of the same race?

Now it may be argued that this would fly in the face of all that Zionism stands for. But even before June fifth the Zionist dream of the state "as Jewish as Britain was British" had not been fulfilled. Even before June fifth Israel had an Arab residue of 300,000, the ones they couldn't evict, the ones who stuck it out, and stayed behind, which was about 15% of the total population. And today Israel occupies an area with nearly a million-and-a-half Arab inhabitants in it; that is almost 40% of the combined population, which scarcely accords with the old Zionist concept of a racially pure Jewish state in the Middle East. Forty per cent Arab! What would the old Zionists say? Thus, whatever final frontiers Israel might, in her present mood of intransigent euphoria be ready to settle for, there will always be, as be there must, a sizeable Arab complement in that area.

But the smaller the area, the less physically able the Israelis will be to resettle Palestine refugees, and Palestine refugee resettlement lies at the heart of any peace settlement with the Arabs. Only the whole of Palestine offers enough scope, given the rate of Jewish settlement both before and after the creation of Israel, and given the natural increase in the numbers of the Palestine refugees. Only the whole of Palestine offers enough scope for a solution of the Palestine refugee problem.

Therefore, I put it to you, if sufficient sanity could be brought to bear upon these issues, it seems that here we have a marriage of necessity and opportunity. The need to solve the problems of the Arabs of Palestine requires the reunification of Palestine and the opportunity to recreate a politically unified Palestine could be seized from the existing situation where Palestine has already been reunified, if only as a geographical entity. Likewise, in the creation of a bi-national state in Palestine lies the best hope of eradicating the suspicion of the Arabs that the sole aim of the West is to create a Western beachhead in the Middle East. The benefits which could flow from this are almost unbelievable and certainly infinite in number.

Yet no one could deny that such a bold step as the offer to recreate a bi-national state in Palestine would require a great act of faith on the part of all concerned. For the Jews to admit so large an Arab minority would require as much courage as for the Arabs to accept to live in a state with so great a Jewish majority. Clearly too, other problems such as the loss of the West Bank to the state of Jordan would also have to be resolved by some economic arrangement with the reconstituted state of Palestine. And there would probably have to be a cooling-off period to allow for tempers to subside, where perhaps the United Nations could help by taking the West Bank under some form of trusteeship until the final arrangements could be worked out to knit together the two parts of Palestine, Jewish and Arab. But if the Jewish people are to find any security in the Middle East then they must live with the Arabs and let the Arabs live with them. *Apartheid,* whether it is practiced in South Africa against the Bantu or in Israel against the Arabs is both as repugnant as it is ultimately impractical.

And however long it takes, and however much it costs, in human effort and financial outlay, it is imperative that a start should be made now along this road and that means the earliest possible initiative by the United States of America with the government of Israel. Mr. President, the alternatives in human suffering and material destruction which a failure to act now could visit upon Jews and Arabs alike are too hideous to contemplate. Today on the fiftieth anniversary of the Balfour Declaration, the Middle East is poised as never before upon the edge of the most awesome precipice. Yet today the Arab world is ready as never before to play its part in settling with Israel on the basis of a just and honorable peace. This, therefore, is probably the best chance that has ever been offered to the peacemakers to end this tragic conflict. But let us be under no illusions: it may well be the last!

2.

THE ARAB-ISRAELI
WAR OF 1967

Charles Woodruff Yost, an American diplomat, was educated at Princeton University and Ecole des Hautes Etudes Internationales, Paris. He was Assistant to the Secretary General of the U. N. at the San Francisco Conference (1945) and Political Advisor to the U. S. Delegation of the U. N. General Assembly (1946). His posts have included ambassadorships to Syria and Morocco. In 1965-66, he served as Deputy Representative to the U. N. Recently named Senior Fellow of the Council of Foreign Relations, Ambassador Yost is author of "The Age of Triumph and Frustration" (1964).

HOW IT BEGAN
Charles W. Yost

The recent Six Day War in the Middle East grew out of
the sterile confrontation to which the peoples of the region
had committed themselves over the past twenty years. Both
parties had frequently proclaimed their intention to go to
war under certain circumstances. It seems unlikely, however,
that any of them plotted and planned war for 1967. It seems
more likely that they blundered into it.

Both sides might on many occasions have moved to end
their confrontation by compromise, but this neither side
showed the slightest willingness to do. The Israelis, feeling
themselves beleaguered by fifty million hostile neighbors,
acutely conscious of the recent fate of six million Jews in
Europe, believed any significant concession would merely whet
insatiable Arab appetites and start Israel down the slippery
slope to extinction. The Arabs, looking upon the establishment of Israel as the latest in a series of imperialist occupa-
tions of their homeland, of which the presence of a million
Palestine refugees was a constant reminder, found it emotionally and politically impossible to accept Israel as a permanent fact of life or to forego harassing it and conspiring
against it.

This common intolerance and mutual harassment had brought on war in 1956. It is pertinent to note that, in his "Diary of the Sinai Campaign" published in 1966, General Dayan wrote that the three major objects of that campaign from the Israeli point of view were "freedom of shipping for Israeli vessels in the Gulf of Aqaba; an end to the Fedayeen terrorism; and a neutralization of the threat of attack on Israel by the joint Egypt-Syria-Jordan military command." With slight variations, these were the issues that brought on war again eleven years later.

Through the latter part of 1966, so-called "El Fatah" incursions into Israel, sometimes carried out by Palestinian refugees, sometimes moving through Jordan or Lebanon, but for the most part mounted in Syria, grew in numbers and intensity. In October two particularly serious incidents in which several Israelis were killed caused Israel to appeal, as it often had before, to the U. N. Security Council. However, a relatively mild resolution proposed by six of its members, calling on Syria to take stronger measures to prevent such incidents, was, as on previous occasions, vetoed by the Soviet Union in the supposed interests of its Arab friends.

A new and more radical Syrian government had come to power by coup d'etat earlier that year. It enthusiastically supported the claims and machinations of the so-called Palestine Liberation Army which mobilized and inflamed the refugees and carried out some of the raids. The Syrian Prime Minister declared in a press conference in October: "We are not sentinels over Israel's security and are not the leash that restrains the revolution of the displaced and persecuted Palestinian people." Early in November, moreover, a "defense agreement" was concluded between Syria and the United Arab Republic, involving a joint military command and other measures of "coordination and integration" between the two countries.

It had long been Israel's practice, whenever it judged that Arab raids had reached an intolerable level, to retaliate massively. It did so on November 13 against Es-Samu in Jordan where, according to U. N. observers, eighteen Jordanian soldiers and civilians were killed and fifty-four wounded. The fact that moderate Jordan rather than extremist Syria was the target of retaliation seemed ill-judged to most of the world but was excused by Israel on grounds that there had recently been thirteen acts of sabotage committed on Israeli territory from Jordanian bases. Be that as it may, the consequences, in and out of the region, of this disproportionate and misplaced retaliation were considerable.

The U. N. Security Council, by a vote of fourteen to one abstention (New Zealand), censured Israel "for this large-scale military action in violation of the U. N. Charter and of the General Armistice Agreement between Israel and Jordan" and emphasized to Israel "that actions of military reprisal cannot be tolerated and that if they are repeated, the Security Council will have to consider further and more effective steps as envisaged in the Charter to ensure against the repetition of such acts."

Perhaps more important in its effect on subsequent events, the Jordanian Prime Minister in a press conference charged the U.A.R. and Syria, which had been denouncing King Hussein's government, with failing to bear their share of the confrontation against Israel. He accused the U.A.R. of failing to supply promised air cover and urged that Egyptian troops be withdrawn from Yemen and sent to Sinai on Israel's southern flank. The U.A.R. Commander-in-Chief of the Arab Command replied publicly with similar recriminations but the charges must have struck home to a regime so peculiarly sensitive to face and prestige.

From January to April 1967 the Syrian-Israeli frontier was agitated by an ascending series of clashes ranging from potshots at tractors plowing to exchanges of fire between tanks, artillery and aircraft. These clashes were primarily caused by the refusal of both sides, at different times, to permit the U.N. Mixed Armistice Commission even to mark the armistice line at disputed points and the insistence of both parties on farming and patrolling disputed areas.

On April 7, 1967, one of these clashes escalated into what in retrospect appears to have been the curtain-raiser to the six-day war. An exchange of fire between tanks gave rise to intervention first by Israeli and then by Syrian aircraft. This led by the end of the day to the appearance of

Israeli planes over the outskirts of Damascus and to the shooting down of six Syrian planes.

The most serious aspect of this affair was that for the second time in six months Arab forces suffered a very bloody nose at the hands of Israel without the "unified Arab Command" in Cairo lifting a finger. President Nasser, who aspired to be leader of the Arab world and who had formally established a military apparatus at least for the containment of Israel, had sat quietly by while first his rival and then his ally had been conspicuously and roundly chastised. Neither the rival nor the ally hesitated publicly and privately to point out this dereliction. Nasser could of course reply, and perhaps did, that the El-Fatah raids were excessive and untimely, that the Arabs must not be provoked into fighting before they were ready, and that the U. N. Emergency Force standing between his army and Israel blocked its coming to the rescue of his Arab allies. These excuses, however genuine and well-founded they may have been, were quite clearly wearing thin in the eyes of the Arabs after the April 7 affair. Those knowing President Nasser's temperament could hardly have felt any assurance that he would hold aloof a third time.

Yet the respite was brief. A month later, on May 11, the U. N. Secretary-General declared at a press luncheon: "I must say that, in the last few days, the El-Fatah type of incidents have increased, unfortunately. Those incidents have occurred in the vicinity of the Lebanese and Syrian lines and are very deplorable, especially because, by their nature, they seem to indicate that the individuals who committed them have had more specialized training than has usually been evidenced in El-Fatah incidents in the past. That type of activity is insidious, is contrary to the letter and spirit of the Armistice Agreements and menaces the peace of the area."

On the same day, May 11, Israeli Prime Minister Eshkol was saying in a public speech in Tel Aviv that his government regarded this wave of sabotage and infiltration gravely. "In view of the fourteen incidents of the past month alone," he said, "we may have to adopt measures no less drastic than those of April 7." In a radio interview two days later he declared: "It is quite clear to the Israeli Government that the focal point of the terrorists is in Syria, but we have laid down the principle that we shall choose the time, the place and the means to counter the aggressor." Eshkol went on to say that he intended to make Israeli defense forces powerful enough to deter aggression, to repel it and to strike a decisive blow within enemy territory.

It would appear that a senior Israeli military officer also made a public comment on or about May 12, the exact text of which it has not been possible to find but which, whether or not correctly understood, significantly contributed to Arab apprehensions. President Nasser referred to it in a speech on May 23, saying, "On May 12 a very important statement was made. . . . The statement said that the Israeli commanders have announced they would carry out military operations against Syria in order to occupy Damascus and overthrow the Syrian Government."

These Israeli exercises in verbal escalation provoked far more serious repercussions than they were no doubt intended to do and, far from sobering the exuberant Syrians and their allies, raised probably genuine fears in Damascus, Cairo and Moscow to a level which brought about the fatal decisions and events of the following week. Indeed the Secretary-General, disturbed that his statement of May 11 on the El-Fatah raids might stimulate Israeli military action, announced on May 13 that that statement "cannot be interpreted as condoning resort to force by any party."

On the same day the Syrian Foreign Ministry summoned ambassadors from countries which were members of the Security Council and told them that a plot against Syria was being concocted by "imperialist and Zionist quarters." The Ministry described "the prearranged aggressive role Israel is preparing to play within the framework of this plot" which, it declared, "began with the abortive April 7 aggression" and was revealed by "statements of Zionist Chief of Staff Rabin."

Another component in the accumulating mass of explosive elements was mentioned by President Nasser in the famous speech of June 9 in which he offered to resign. He declared at that time: "We all know how the crisis began in the first half of last May. There was a plan by the enemy to invade Syria, and the statements by his politicians and his military commanders declared that frankly. The evidence was ample. The sources of our Syrian brothers and our own reliable information were categorical on this. Even our friends in the Soviet Union told the parliamentary delegation which was visiting Moscow last month that there was a calculated intention."

There seems little doubt that the Soviets did transmit warnings along these lines to the Syrian and Egyptian governments. Eastern European sources have justified these warnings on the grounds that the Israeli Government itself advised Soviet representatives that, if the El-Fatah raids continued, it would take drastic punitive action against Syria. This was of course no more than they were saying publicly, but the Israelis may have hoped that direct notice to the Soviets might induce them to persuade their Syrian friends to stop the raids.

Indeed there is evidence that Israeli officials were at this time disseminating their warnings rather widely. *The New York Times* correspondent, James Feron, in Tel Aviv reported on May 12: "Some Israeli leaders have decided that the use of force against Syria may be the only way to curtail increasing terrorism. Any such Israeli reaction to continued infiltration would be of considerable strength but of short duration and limited in area. This has become apparent in talks with highly qualified and informed Israelis who have spoken in recent days against a background of mounting border violence."

However, these private warnings, coupled with the provocative pronouncements by Eshkol and others, would seem to have backfired by convincing the Soviets, Syrians and Egyptians that a major retaliatory strike against Syria was fixed and imminent. In a speech to the United Nations on June 19 Premier Kosygin declared: "In those days, the Soviet Government, and I believe others too, began receiving information to the effect that the Israeli Government had timed for the end of May a swift strike at Syria in order to crush it and then carry the fighting over into the territory of the United Arab Republic."

On the other hand, the Israelis state that on May 12 the Director General of the Israeli Foreign Ministry, on May 19 the Foreign Minister and on May 29 the Prime Minister each invited Soviet Ambassador Chuvakhin, who had accused Israel of massing forces on the Syrian border, to visit the area and see for himself, but that in each case he refused to do so. Furthermore, in his report to the Security Council on May 19, Secretary-General Thant had referred to allegations about troop movements and concentrations on the Israeli side of the Syrian border but concluded: "Reports from UNTSO observers have confirmed the absence of troop concentrations and significant troop movements on both sides of the line." U. S. representatives in Israel at the time also saw no evidence of the alleged troop concentrations. Moreover, on May 15 the Israeli Government, observing that Egyptian forces were crossing the Suez Canal into Sinai in considerable strength, instructed its Representative at the U. N., Ambassador Rafael, to request the Secretary-General to assure Cairo on its behalf that it had no intention of initiating any military action. The Secretary-General immediately complied with the request.

Nevertheless, it should also be noted that in the May 19 report referred to above the Secretary-General remarked: "Intemperate and bellicose utterances . . . are unfortunately more or less routine on both sides of the lines in the Near East. In recent weeks, however, reports emanating from Israel have attributed to some high officials in that state statements so threatening as to be particularly inflammatory in the sense that they could only heighten emotions and thereby increase tensions on the other side of the lines." Press accounts of these statements also seemed so inflammatory to U. S. State Department officials that they expressed concern to Israeli authorities.

The situation in mid-May was therefore the following: the aggravation of the El-Fatah raids originating in Syria would seem to have brought the Israeli Government to the decision, announced publicly in general terms by responsible officals and confided in more specific terms to journalists and perhaps to foreign diplomats including the Soviets, to retaliate sharply and substantially if the raids continued.

There is no solid evidence, however, that they intended anything so massive as a drive on Damascus. Nevertheless, this prospect had in both Moscow and Cairo an impact which the Israelis probably did not fully anticipate or correctly assess.

The Soviets had particular reason for not wishing to see the Syrian Government humiliated, defeated and perhaps overthrown. The increasingly radical Syrian governments which had assumed power during the previous eighteen months, though they were far from being communist (the Communist Party was and still is banned), had come to rely more and more on Soviet military and economic aid, to permit increasing numbers of Soviet advisers to be stationed in the country, and all in all to offer the most promising field for Soviet penetration and influence to be found anywhere in the Middle East. The particular Soviet concern for Syria was dramatically shown at the end of the six-day war when the prospect that Israeli forces might then drive to Damascus caused the Soviets suddenly to join in a demand, which they had up to that point stubbornly opposed, that U. N. observers police the cease-fire. It may well have been that by mid-May they genuinely feared massive Israeli retaliation which might topple the Syrian Government and that they therefore spurred the Egyptians on to vigorous counteraction, the full repercussions of which they did not foresee. In fear of "losing" Syria they overreached themselves and urged the Arabs to take action which resulted in much more disastrous losses for their side.

Nasser, for his part, saddled with responsibility for the unified Arab Command which was supposed to protect all the Arab states from Israel, jealous of his already damaged position as would-be leader of the Arab world, having been ridiculed by his allies and rivals for his failure to stir at the time of the Es-Samu and April 7 affairs, categorically assured by Syrians and Soviets that Israel was about to attack Syria, for which public statements by Israeli leaders seemed to give warrant, may well have felt that he could no longer stand aside without fatal loss to his prestige and authority.

Israeli public statements between May 11 and 13, therefore, regardless of how they may have been intended, may well have been the spark that ignited the long accumulating tinder. On May 14 the Egyptian Chief of Staff flew to Damascus and, according to the Syrian official spokesman, discussed with Syrian officials "important matters concerning joint defense against Israel." On May 16 the Cairo radio announced that the United Arab Republic had declared a state of emergency for its armed forces because of "the tense situation on the Syrian-Israeli armistice lines, Israel's large military concentrations, its threats and its open demands for an attack on Damascus." On that same day, according to the Cairo radio, Foreign Minister Riad received the Soviet, Syrian and Iraqi Ambassadors in separate audiences and Minister of War Badran received the Soviet Ambassador accompanied by his military attache. The fourth act of the tragedy was about to begin.

At 2200 hours local time that evening, May 16, General Rikhye, Commander of the U. N. Emergency Force in Sinai, was handed the following letter from General Fawzi, Chief of Staff of the Egyptian Armed Forces: "To your information, I gave my instructions to all U.A.R. Armed Forces to be ready for action against Israel the moment it might carry out an aggressive action against any Arab country. Due to these instructions our troops are already concentrated in Sinai on our eastern borders. For the sake of complete security of all U. N. troops which install O.P.s along our border, I request that you issue your orders to withdraw all these troops immediately. I have given my instructions to our Commander of the eastern zone concerning this subject. Inform back the fulfillment of this request."

Secretary-General Thant received General Rikhye's report at 1730 hours New York time that same evening and an hour and a quarter later (at 1845 hours) at his urgent request received the U.A.R. representative to the U. N., Ambassador El-Kony, to whom he presented the following views: (1) General Rikhye could not take orders from anyone but the Secretary-General; (2) if General Fawzi was asking for a temporary withdrawal of UNEF from the Line this was unacceptable because UNEF "cannot be asked to stand aside in order to enable the two sides to resume fighting"; (3) if General Fawzi was asking for a general withdrawal of UNEF from Gaza and Sinai the request should have been addressed by the U.A.R. Government to the Secretary-General; (4) the U.A.R. Government had the right "to withdraw the consent which it gave in 1956 for the stationing of UNEF on the territory of the U.A.R."; (5) if the U.A.R. Government addressed such a request to the Secretary-General he "would order the withdrawal of all UNEF troops from Gaza and Sinai, simultaneously informing the General Assembly of what he was doing and why"; (6) a U.A.R. request for a temporary withdrawal of UNEF from the Line would be considered by the Secretary-General "as tantamount to a request for the complete withdrawal of UNEF from Gaza and Sinai, since this would reduce UNEF to ineffectiveness."

Early the next morning, May 17, Egyptian troops began to move into and beyond some UNEF positions along the Armistice Line. At noon G.M.T. that day General Fawzi conveyed to General Rikhye a request that the Jugo-slav detachments of UNEF (which occupied the main portion of the Sinai Armistice Line) be withdrawn within 24 hours, adding, however, that the UNEF Commander might take "24 hours or so" to withdraw the UNEF detachment from Sharm el Sheikh (which commands the Straits of Tiran but is far distant from the Armistice Line).

Space permits only the briefest summary of the events which followed in rapid succession. On the afternoon of May 17 in New York the Secretary-General consulted with representatives of countries providing contingents to UNEF (Brazil, Canada, Denmark, India, Jugoslavia, Norway and Sweden). According to his subsequent report to the General Assembly, two of them expressed serious doubts about complying with "a peremptory request" for withdrawal and suggested reference to the Assembly, whereas two others maintained the United Arab Republic had the right to request withdrawal at any time and that request would have to be respected regardless of what the Assembly might say. Later that afternoon the Secretary-General presented to the U.A.R. Representative an aide-memoire reiterating the points he had made the previous evening and concluding that, if Egyptian troop movements up to the Line were maintained, he would "have no choice but to order the withdrawal of UNEF from Gaza and Sinai as expeditiously as possible."

The next morning, May 18, Foreign Minister Riad informed representatives in Cairo of nations with troops in UNEF that "UNEF had terminated its tasks in the U.A.R. and in the Gaza Strip and must depart from the above territory forthwith." At noon New York time the Secretary-General received a formal request from the Egyptian Foreign Minister to the same effect. That afternoon he met with the UNEF Advisory Committee where he encountered the same divergence of views as at the meeting the previous day but where the members finally acquiesced in his belief that, in the absence of any proposal to convene the Assembly, he "had no alternative other than to comply with the U.A.R.'s demand." He did so that same evening by a message to Foreign Minister Riad and by instructions to the UNEF Commander.

The immediate reaction of Israel also deserves mention. On the morning of May 18 the Secretary-General received the Israeli representative who presented his Government's view "that the UNEF withdrawal should not be achieved by a unilateral U.A.R. request alone and asserting Israel's right to a voice in the matter." When, however, the Secretary-General raised the possibility of stationing UNEF on the Israeli side of the line, the Representative replied that this would be "entirely unacceptable to his Government," thus reaffirming the position in regard to UNEF which Israel had taken ever since the establishment of the Force in 1956.

The intent and rationale of the decisions taken in Cairo during those critical days in mid-May are still shrouded in obscurity, while those taken in response in New York are still bedeviled by controversy. What seems reasonably clear is that, as so often in the prelude to war, the control of events slipped from everyone's hands and limited decisions hastily taken had sweeping consequences no one desired.

No doubt the Egyptian Government decided sometime between May 13 and 16 that, in view of its assessment of the threat to Syria, it must move some of its armed forces up to the Sinai Armistice Line in order either to deter Israel or to come to Syria's assistance if deterrence failed. Reliable Arab sources maintain that: (1) the U.A.R. Government had as late as May 16 no intention to request the withdrawal of UNEF; (2) it desired merely the removal of several UNEF posts along the Sinai Line which would inhibit the contemplated redeployment of Egyptian forces; (3) it saw no incompatibility between this redeployment and the continuance of UNEF in its other positions *including* Sharm el-Sheikh; (4) the implementation of the redevelopment was left to the military leaders who failed to consult the civilian authorities, including the President, about either the scope of the redeployment they intended to carry out or the demand addressed to General Rikhye on May 16; (5) when the Secretary-General confronted the U.A.R. Government with the naked choice between reversing the redeployment, to which its military leaders had publicly committed it, and requesting the withdrawal of UNEF, it felt obliged to choose the latter; (6) furthermore, when it unexpectedly found its forces once more in possession of Sharm el Sheikh, it felt it could not fail to exercise, as it had from 1954 to 1956, its "belligerent right" to forbid the passage of Israeli vessels and "war material" through the Strait.

As to the decisions taken in New York, the U.N. authorities have maintained that: (1) the indicated redeployment of U.A.R. forces *was* incompatible with the continuance of UNEF since it deprived UNEF of its essential function as a buffer between Egyptian and Israeli forces; (2) UNEF had hitherto been able to function effectively only because of an informal U.A.R. agreement that its forces would be held 2,000 meters back from the Armistice Line in Sinai (Israeli forces patrolled right up to the Line); (3) once confrontation between the two forces was re-established, conflict between them was, in the existing state of tension, very probable and UNEF units scattered among them would be wholly unable to prevent it; (4) two of the troop-contributing states, India and Jugoslavia, had made clear their intention to withdraw their contingents whatever the Secretary-General decided and others were likely to follow suit, with the probable result that UNEF would dis-integrate in a disordered and ignominious fashion; (5) the U.A.R. Government had the legal right both to move its troops where it wished in its own territory and to insist on the withdrawal of UNEF at any time, just as Israel had the right to refuse it admittance; (6) if the U. N. contested that right, peacekeeping would become "occupation" and other governments would not in the future admit U. N. peace-keeping forces to their territories; (7) a reference of the Egyptian request to the Security Council or the Assembly would merely have produced, as subsequent events proved, a prolonged debate during which UNEF would have either disintegrated or been helplessly involved in war.

No conclusive judgment can be pronounced on these two lines of argument. What does seem apparent is that both the U.A.R. and the U. N., like Israel a few days before, acted precipitately and with little resort to diplomacy. If the Egyptian account is accurate, temporization on the part of the U. N. might conceivably have led to some modification in U.A.R. military dispositions which had not been authorized by its own government. It seems very doubtful, however, that in the prevailing state of emotion dispositions once taken, even without full authorization, could have been reversed. By May 17 the crisis had already acquired a momentum which seemed inexorably to sweep all parties toward and over the brink.

Nevertheless, we can hardly fail to note parenthetically the serious shortcomings of a peacekeeping procedure whereby, as in this case, a U. N. force can be ordered out of a critical area at the very moment when the danger of war, which it is stationed there to prevent, becomes most acute. The fault, however, lies not with the U. N. but with the great powers whose rivalries ever since 1945 have blocked the application of the enforcement procedures provided by Chapter VII of the Charter, under which a U. N. military force could be, for example, interposed between two prospective combatants regardless of the objections of either or both. In the absence of great-power willingness to permit the Security Council to apply compulsion of that type, the U. N. has been obliged for many years to rely on a much more fragile form of peacekeeping whereunder a U.N. force, whatever may have been the arrangements under which it entered the territory of a state, can in practice remain there only so long as its government consents. Such was the situation in Sinai before May 16.

To return to the concluding events of that month: President Nasser on May 22 announced his intention to reinstitute the blockade against Israel in the Strait of Tiran. This was the final fatal step. Whether, in whatever advance planning did take place, it was contemplated that Sharm el Sheikh would be reoccupied and the blockade reimposed, or whether the military exceeded their orders and one step led to another in dizzy and unpremeditated succession, is not certain. There can hardly have been any doubt at any time, however, about the grave risks involved in restoring the blockade. It seems probable that the Russians were consulted about the redeployment of Egyptian forces and perhaps the subsequent request for the withdrawal of UNEF. Reliable Soviet sources have claimed, however, that they were not informed in advance of the reimposition of the blockade, implying that they would have objected had they known.

In any case, the reaction in Israel and elsewhere was immediate. On May 23 Prime Minister Eshkol declared in parliament: "The Knesset knows that any interference with freedom of shipping in the Gulf and in the Straits constitutes a flagrant violation of international law. . . . It constitutes an act of aggression against Israel." On the same day President Johnson declared in Washington: "The United States considers the Gulf to be an international waterway and feels that a blockade of Israeli shipping is illegal and potentially disastrous to the cause of peace. The right of free, innocent passage of the international waterway is a vital interest of the international community."

Unavailing efforts were made to persuade President Nasser to revoke, suspend or moderate the blockade but, the action once taken, he did not feel politically free to reverse it, even had he so desired. Equally unavailing were efforts made to forestall a unilateral Israeli response by organizing a group of maritime powers to issue a declaration reaffirming the right of free passage through the Strait and presumably, if passage continued to be denied, to take effective multilateral action to reopen it. Very few maritime powers showed any interest in participating in a confrontation with Nasser and the Arab world, nor did members of the U. S. Congress who were consulted manifest any enthusiasm for risking another conflict in addition to Viet Nam. The exploratory dialogue between the U. S. and the U.A.R., however, continued up until the outbreak of war; as late as June 4 an agreement was announced that U.A.R. Vice President Mohieddin would visit Washington within the next few days and Vice President Humphrey would later return the visit.

In the meantime, however, the crisis had assumed proportions far beyond an argument over maritime rights. The advance of the Egyptian forces to the Armistice Line, the ouster of UNEF and the reimposition of the blockade were received with enormous enthusiasm throughout the Arab world. All the pent-up emotions which had been accumulating for twenty years, and which were continually refreshed by armed clashes, inflammatory propaganda and the presence of a million refugees, erupted in paeans of triumph from Baghdad to Marrakesh.

Nasser's prestige, which had been falling for some time, rebounded overnight. Expressions of solidarity poured in. Iraq, Algeria, Kuwait and Sudan promised troops. In a startling reversal of long-standing hostility, King Hussein of Jordan appeared in Cairo on May 30 and concluded a mutual defense pact with the U.A.R. which a few days later was extended to Iraq. The armed forces of Egypt, Jordan and Syria were more and more concentrated around Israel's frontiers and there seemed every likelihood they would soon be reinforced by other Arab states.

This Arab euphoria, moreover, led also to verbal exaltation which could not have been without its effect on Israel. For instance, the Syrian Chief of State, Dr. Al-Atasi, said in a speech on May 22: "Arab Palestinians who were expelled from their homeland now realize that armed struggle is the only way to regain their homeland. . . . The state of gangs (Israel) will not benefit by blaming others for inciting fedayeen activities. The cause of these activities is the aggressive Zionist existence itself. Let Israel know that the Palestinian fedayeen activities will continue until they liberate their homeland." In a speech addressed on June 1 to troops departing for the "frontlines" in Jordan, President Arif of Iraq declared: "It was treason and politics that brought about the creation of Israel. Brethren and sons, this is the day of the battle to revenge your martyred brethren who fell in 1948. It is the day to wash away the stigma. We shall, God willing, meet in Tel Aviv and Haifa."

Yet even at this late date, despite all these verbal pyrotechnics and concentrations of force, there does not seem to have been any intention in Cairo to initiate a war. In reply to a question by British M. P. Christopher Mayhew interviewing Nasser on June 2, "And if they do not attack, will you let them alone?", the President said, "Yes, we will leave them alone. We have no intention of attacking Israel." Similar assurances were repeatedly given the United States by the highest Egyptian authorities.

There seems little reason to doubt them. Nasser had up to that point achieved a spectacular victory. Arab unity seemed closer to reality than it had ever been. Israel had suffered a serious set-back in prestige, power and security. The mood in Cairo was an odd mixture of exaltation and fatalism, exaltation over what had been achieved, fatalism before the inescapable realization that Israel might prefer war to a political defeat of this magnitude. There was a clear understanding that Israel might attack at any time, no overweening confidence as to the outcome, but a determination to defend, whatever the costs, the intoxicating gains which had been won. Whether this determination might have been overcome by negotiation over a period of time, for example by the visits of the Vice Presidents between Cairo and Washington, cannot be known for certain. In view of the support which the Soviet Union was providing its Arab friends, this seems unlikely.

In any case the Israeli Government obviously decided that it could not wait. All the factors which had induced it to go to war in 1956—a multiplication of raids into its territory, a substantial build-up of Egyptian and other hostile forces on its borders, the blockade of the Strait—had re-appeared in even more aggravated form. Efforts of the U.N. and the U.S. to relieve them by international action seemed unavailing. On May 30 Foreign Minister Eban said in a press conference in Jerusalem: "Less than two weeks ago a change took place in the security balance in this region. The two most spectacular signs of this change were the illegal attempt to blockade the international passageway at the Strait of Tiran and the Gulf of Aqaba and the abnormal buildup of Egyptian troops on the Israeli frontier. The Government and people of Israel intend to insure that these two changes are rescinded, and in the shortest possible time." Six days later Israel struck with this end in view; twelve days later it had achieved its objective, and much more beside.

It is not difficult in retrospect to identify the ventures and responses on both sides which over preceding months and weeks, compounding the hatreds which had been allowed to fester for twenty years, led almost inevitably to war.

First were the El-Fatah raids, organized from Syria, involving the "Palestine Liberation Army," subjecting peaceful Israeli villages to recurrent jeopardy and terror, building up through the months from October to May, unpunished and, because of the Soviet veto, even uncensured by the U.N. Security Council. Remembering the history of the previous twelve years, it is difficult to see how any Arab or Soviet leader could have failed to realize that this murderous campaign would eventually bring forth a murderous response.

Second were the Israeli "massive retaliations" at Es-Samu in November and in the air over Syria and Jordan in April, designed to punish and deter, but disproportionate in size, visibility and political impact, causing also the death of innocent people, condemned by the Security Council in the strongest terms in November, as similar disproportionate retaliations had been repeatedly condemned in the past. It is difficult to see how any Israeli leader could have failed to foresee that such repeated massive reprisals must eventually place the leader of the Arab coalition in a position where he would have to respond.

87

Third were the public and private statements by high Israeli authorities in mid-May which indicated the probability of even more drastic retaliation against Syria in the near future if the El-Fatah raids continued. These statements, even though no doubt designed to deter the raids, almost certainly convinced the Syrian and U.A.R. Governments that such retaliation was definitely projected and may well have persuaded them and the Soviets that the Syrian regime itself was in jeopardy.

Fourth was the decision by the U.A.R. Government, presumably encouraged by Soviets and Syrians, to move its armed forces up to the Sinai Armistice Line, thus reestablishing at a moment of acute tension the direct Egyptian-Israeli military confrontation which had been the major immediate cause of the 1956 war. This redeployment of Egyptian forces was under the circumstances critical whether or not it was originally intended to be accompanied by a demand that UNEF be withdrawn.

Fifth and finally was the decision of the U.A.R. Government, finding itself whether by intent or accident once more in command of the Strait of Tiran, to exercise its "belligerent rights" by reimposing the blockade, thus reproducing the third of the elements which had brought on the 1956 war. The likely consequences of this step were indeed foreseen but, in the climate of fear, passion and "national honor" which by then prevailed, were faced with fatalism and desperation.

It remains, however, the thesis of this article that no government plotted or intended to start a war in the Middle East in the spring of 1967. Syria mounted raids against Israel as it had been doing for years, but more intensively and effectively; Israel retaliated disproportionately as it often had before, but in more rapid succession and in a way that seemed to threaten the existence of the Arab government; Nasser felt his responsibilities and ambitions in the Arab world did not permit him again to stand aside in such a contingency and took hasty and ill-calculated measures which made major conflict, already probable, practically certain. All concerned overreacted outrageously. Yet there is no evidence—quite the contrary—that either Nasser or the Israeli

Government or even the Syrian Government wanted and sought a major war at this juncture.

Of course the fault of all of them, and indeed of the great powers and the United Nations, lay not so much in their actions or omissions in May and June 1967 as in their failure, indeed their common blunt refusal, to face the facts of life in the Middle East during the twenty years before that date.

There will be no peace there, no security for its inhabitants or for the great powers involved there, until the Arabs recognize that Israel, however unjust its creation appears to them, is a fact of life, that it has as much right to exist as they have, that to threaten and harass it, to arouse among their people false hopes about its dissolution, is actually as much a threat to Arab as to Israeli security, that the two equally have more to gain than lose by peaceful coexistence. On the other hand, there will also be no peace in the Middle East until the Israelis recognize that the condition of their long-term survival as a nation is reconciliation with their much more numerous Arab neighbors, that survival cannot indefinitely be preserved by military force or territorial expansion, that displays of inflexibility and arrogance are not effective modes of international intercourse, and that in particular there will be no security for Israel until, whatever the political and financial cost, the million or more Palestine refugees have been compensated, resettled and restored to dignity.

Washington might undertake—and that our support would not go beyond that.

When it appeared that the Israelis considered the blockade of the Gulf of Aqaba as a *casus belli* and that the situation had become grave, the hot line between Washington and Moscow began operating. Kosygin and Johnson agreed to work on their allies—the one on Egypt and Syria, the other on Israel—in order to prevent them from resorting to arms. They also decided to keep military forces out of the theater of operations, to take the measures necessary to avoid contact between these forces and to immediately get in touch should an incident occur so that it would not degenerate into a serious conflict. (This is why Washington promptly notified us when planes took off from the Sixth Fleet after an American vessel had been attacked through an error by the Israelis.)

Nasser, knowing our reservations, promised he would not be the first to attack, but he committed the error of believing that the agreement between the two big powers allowed him all the time he needed for diplomatic maneuvers. In fact, he was partially a victim of his own propaganda which claimed that the Tel Aviv Government was merely Washington's pawn. He did not want to believe that this pawn might act on its own. Furthermore, he made a major mistake in neglecting the military side of the crisis. It did not even occur to him to put his airfields in a state of alert. This lack of foresight (or sabotage by some top officers hostile to Nasser) caused the destruction of the excellent military material we had given Egypt. The truth is we had overrated the ability of the commanding staff and logistics of the Egyptian military apparatus. Since 1956, the Egyptian Army units up to battalion level had made great progress in terms of courage and maneuverability, but the shortcomings above this level turned out to be shocking.

The second exchange on the hot line between Johnson and Kosygin dealt with an American proposal for a general settlement of the Middle East problem. Wanting to protect their oil interests on the Arab peninsula and their political positions in Jordan, the Americans proposed to settle the question of freedom of navigation in the Gulf of Aqaba by a compromise between the Israeli and Arab viewpoints. The Israelis would be compensated by substantial economic and financial aid from the United States, and a large-scale plan of economic aid similar to that which had been projected for the "Alliance for Progress" in Latin America would be launched for the benefit of all the Arab countries, including Egypt and Syria. The Soviet Union was invited to make a parallel effort. Kosygin replied that he needed more facts, but that *a priori* he was not opposed to this project. In order to test the reactions of the Egyptians to the plan, Johnson invited one of the men closest to Nasser, Zakaria Mohieddin, to come to Washington. On our advice, Mohieddin accepted the invitation which only strengthened Nasser's convictions that hostilities would not erupt. In addition, the Israelis skillfully hoodwinked him. At the very moment when Dayan was making the final preparations for his lightning offensive, he stated at a press conference that his country would not attack first. But in fact the Israelis had decided to act and confront the world with the *fait accompli* of their military victory.

The drama unfolded at dawn on Monday, June 5. Almost all of the Jordanian and Syrian air forces and two-thirds of the Egyptian air force were destroyed on the ground. Dramatic conversations took place in Cairo between Nasser and our ambassador and in Moscow between the Egyptian Ambassador and the top members of the Soviet collective leadership which had been called into an emergency meeting. The Egyptians demanded that we, the Soviets, immediately replace their destroyed airforce. But where were the new craft to be landed? All the Egyptian airfields were under fire by Israeli planes except Luxor and Aswan in Upper Egypt, and these fields were poorly equipped to handle such attacks. The Egyptians suggested sending the planes to the Sudan, to Iraq or to Libya; we refused because the two or three airfields in the Sudan and Iraq are small and inadequate. As for sending Soviet planes into Libya, a few miles from the American base, Wheelus Field, Washington would regard it as a provocation—and we did not want war with the United States.

The dialogues between the Egyptians and us grew

strained. They accused us of abandoning them in the hour of need. We replied that we had committed ourselves to supporting them against American action but not against Israel, whose power they had underestimated. After the success of the Israeli offensive we decided, without consulting the Egyptians, that we could accept an immediate cease-fire in the Security Council because the Arab positions on the ground were still not catastrophic. De Gaulle, who was in communication with Kosygin, shared our view.

The Egyptians mistakenly believed they could take the first punch thrown by the Israelis in ground fighting. Once that danger had passed, they would begin a long war which they could win due to the large area and numerical superiority of the Arab world. We told them they were substituting their wishes for realities since their tanks would be beaten without air cover. Nasser did not want to believe us and launched his counter-offensive, which failed. He closed the door on the only reasonable solution: to pay the price in ground fighting under the least disadvantageous conditions possible and gain precious time during which he would be able to quietly rebuild his air force.

As Nasser continued his desperate struggle, we became aware that the Arab world and a large part of the Third World, not to mention the Chinese, disapproved of the inadequacy of our support to Egypt. Suddenly, some of our leaders began thinking of taking the risk of limited military action on behalf of Egypt within the framework of a "prudent challenge" to the United States. However, this solution was finally rejected. (As elsewhere, the pressure of Jewish opinion made its weight felt in the U.S.S.R. right up to the leading circles.)

The latest events prove the imperialism of Israeli policy and our attitude toward Tel Aviv is going to get even tougher. The Israelis are now the mad dogs of the Middle East. You don't kill a mad dog because he has a right to live, but you do have to punish him. We now firmly believe this punishment is required to bring Israel to its senses and that undoubtedly it will take place some day. The Israelis have pointed out the road the Arabs must take:

94

to launch a surprise air attack one day on the vulnerable territory of tiny Israel.

The political and diplomatic struggle we are going to wage alongside the Arabs, especially the Syrians and Nasser, will be difficult. As for the Americans, we shall exploit to the utmost the blackmailing of their oil interests and navigation through the Suez Canal.

We shall fight at all the conference tables to force the Israelis to evacuate the territories they conquered. And we shall wage an incessant propaganda war, particularly among the young Arab generation, against all the cowards, opportunists and elements linked to the Anglo-Americans who show any readiness to cooperate with Israel—as long as Israel does not agree to the concessions that we shall demand of her.

We know that our prestige has suffered terribly among the Arabs. The most intelligent will come to understand that it was impossible for us to act otherwise. When reason finally prevails over emotions, the progressive Arab leaders will have to admit that if the Americans are now the target of spontaneous, vigilant hatred in the Arab world, there is only one great power that can help the Arabs recover from the disaster—the Soviet Union. One may say that the big winner in this crisis has been Mao Tse-tung. But let's be serious: who can pull Egypt and Syria out of the hornet's nest, and, to start with, rebuild their air forces? The Chinese?

Professor John S. Badeau, Director of the Middle East Institute at Columbia University, lived in the Arab world from 1928 to 1953 and again from 1961 until mid-1964, while serving as American Ambassador to the United Arab Republic. For seventeen years he was variously Professor, Dean, and President at the American University in Cairo.

THE ARABS, 1967

John S. Badeau

As the dust of battle settled over Sinai after six brief days of fighting, only the spoor of fleeing Arab forces remained to mark the tragic Arab-Israeli conflict of June, 1967. Yet though the victory was swift and irrevocable, it has not yet proved decisive. Will stunning defeat bring the Arabs to their moment of truth, marking the beginning of the end of their hostility toward Israel? Or may it be the end of the beginning of Israel's existence, ushering in a Hundred Years' War in which the rising tide of Arab population and resources ultimately will engulf the tiny state? These questions cannot now be answered; much will depend upon the accuracy and realism with which the causes of the recent struggle are appraised and their lessons applied to the future.

In the immediate aftermath of conflict, there has been a tendency to oversimplify and emotionalize the issues, reducing them to terms of innocence and blame which absolve each party from responsibility in its own eyes. To both sides and their supporters, the key lies in "aggression," that portmanteau word which modern man must eschew since it is not respectable to admit anything but "defensive"

97

military action. Thus the Arabs claim their action was "defensive" since (they maintain) Israel fired the shot and launched the invasion which precipitated war. Israel points to the closing of the Gulf of Aqaba as the *casus belli,* to which their military action was only a defensive response. Which was the true cause for the outbreak of war?

The answer must be that neither was; what broke out in overt conflict was the surfacing of disputes and policies to which each contestant had long contributed. On their part, the Arabs had persistently underestimated the reality and predictability of Israel's reaction to nineteen years of unrelenting hostility by the encircling Arab world. Faced with a sustained state of belligerency, the target of constant threats and innuendos, beset with intermittent border raids and terrorist attacks, Israel could not be counted upon to

exercise restraint under mounting provocation—as any perceptive Arab leader should have known. No state can acquiesce in a permanent threat to its existence, no government can abdicate its responsibility to protect the lives and property of its citizens from attack. Sustained periods of guerrilla terrorism, such as that which began in the summer of 1966, would inevitably generate a sharp Israeli reaction, and the Arabs have only themselves to blame if they failed to recognize this.

That they consistently underestimated the temper of Israel is due in part to the difference between the credibility of Arab and Israeli statements of intent. The Arab world is highly verbal; words are often ends in themselves and not necessarily forerunners of action. The fact that an Arab leader states a purpose publicly is not an invariable sign that he will carry it out, as the shrill crescendo of verbal inter-Arab warfare during the past few years clearly shows. Too often the Arabs tended to give the same weight to Israeli statements that they gave to their own, to their dismay when prompt action followed.

Moreover, Arab estimates of Israeli intentions were affected by their conviction that the great powers (especially the United States) really controlled the country; hence Israel would not make a major move without foreign support and acquiescence, if not with actual urging. The possibility of Israeli armed action thus went beyond what Israel itself might purpose and be capable of doing, involving estimates of what the West would allow Israel to do. The immediate and universal Arab acceptance of the fiction that American planes assisted Israel in its attack against the U.A.R. was due in part to the belief that Israel could not have undertaken military action without the encouragement and support of the United States—hence it appeared credible that American planes were dispatched to help Israel. This seemed the more logical in view of the long history of American commitments and arms sales to Israel, and the flood of public statements across the years from leading American personalities and politicians giving uncritical support to Israel's cause. *128/35*

But the Arab action which led to the 1967 conflict had deeper roots. The reasons for sustained Arab hostility toward Israel are more profound and intricate than many Americans allow themselves to believe. Such simple answers as "Arabs hate Jews," "the backward Arab world fears the existence of a modern and democratic state in its midst," "the Arabs in general do not feel deeply about Israel, it is their leaders who whip up enmity for their own purposes" not only explain nothing, but are untrue. Such shallow estimates of Arab motivation have led many supporters of Israel to underestimate the depth and stamina of the Arab response and to be oversanguine that a determined display of force will lead to peace. The question is not one of accepting the Arab point of view, but of understanding it, so that approaches and policies will be grounded in realism and not in wishful thinking. If the Arabs have persistently, and to their hurt, underestimated the fact of Israel's existence and its predictable response to their enmity, Israel and its supporters have as persistently, and to their hurt, underestimated the facts of Arab feelings and the problems Israel's existence poses for them.

The outbreak of conflict in the spring of 1967, after nine years of relative peace, encapsuled the principal elements in the Arab attitude toward Israel. Its most basic lesson is that Arab hostility is still bitter and ubiquitous after nearly two decades of fruitless struggle. In many ways, 1967 was not a repetition of 1956, when the Egyptian response to Israel's invasion of its territory was a limited action and did not precipitate general Arab war. It was rather a return to 1948, when the Arabs fought as a group against the existence of Israel as a country. It is this fact which has baffled and angered so many who support Israel. They feel it is irrational and irresponsible for a people to continue hostility so long and in the face of such repeated failure. By this time the Arabs should have made their peace with events and come to terms with what they could not undo. That they have not done so, the argument runs, must be due to an irrational streak in their temperament, to the cynical machinations of their leaders, to irradicable anti-Jewism, or to the scheming of the Soviet Union.

Yet of all people, the Jewish community should understand the tenacity of racial memory and long-sustained feeling. Through the years of dispersion, they never forgot Palestine, although it was only since the last century that this steadfastness involved dedication to the re-creation of a Jewish state in the long-remembered homeland.

This is not to say that the factors involved in the Jewish attachment to Israel are precisely the same as those contained in the Arab sense of connection with Palestine. Palestine was not the original historical center of life and religion for the Arabs, as it was for Jewry. The Arabs were not a minority dispersed through many lands, and they did not suffer under discrimination and persecution, as many Jews had. They never faced a threat of racial extinction, as European Jews did under Nazism, in which a national refuge became a matter of life and death for many. Although Palestine had been an Arab land since at least the seventh century and contained important religious sites (both Christian and Muslim), it did not fill the horizon of Arab consciousness, as it did for many Jews. Why then is the Arab connection with Palestine so strong and the sense of outrage at its loss so deep?

The most basic cause is found in the intense Arab reaction against long-continued domination of their destinies by foreign countries. In the fading days of Ottoman rule, the Arab communities of the Middle East were stirred by nationalistic consciousness akin to that involved in the emergence of the Zionist ideal in Jewry. They sought cultural revival, political expression, and community selfhood within the body of the Turkish Empire—a recognition of "Arabistan" as an entity in which the destiny of the Arab people could be achieved. Thwarted in their struggle, some of their principal leaders responded to British promises during the First World War and joined the Allies in the overthrow of Ottoman rule. They did so on the understanding that their national aspirations would be recognized and some form of independent Arab rule achieved.

In recent days there have been repeated references to the statement of Faisal (a principal leader of the Arab Revolt in 1916-1918 and later King of Iraq) that there was no conflict between the aims of Zionism and Arab nationalism. Those who quote it leave out the essential condition which Faisal attached to his statement, that *all the promises made to the Arabs should be fulfilled.* This was not done; the attempt to create an Arab state was checkmated by France and Great Britain, who carved up the Arab portion of the defunct Ottoman Empire to suit their own purposes. The creation of Iraq, Syria, modern Lebanon, Jordan, and (mandated) Palestine was not a fulfillment of Arab independence, but the parceling out of Arab populations to suit the convenience of the victorious Allied Powers.

The Arabs never forgot this. It was the Great Betrayal of their national cause, the incontestable proof that the West meant to divide and rule them in its own interests. After two decades of sharp struggle between individual nationalisms in Arab countries and their Western masters, the Second World War came to erode imperial ties and create a new organ of international action. Arab nationalism took new hope and looked forward to becoming at last the master of its own destiny.

It was at this juncture that the creation of Israel was forced on the Arab world. The plea that Nazi persecution justified the creation did not move the Arabs, since these persecutions were the product of anti-Semitism in the Western world and not in the Middle East, where Arab-Jewish

101

relations had been remarkably good. "It was the West which persecuted the Jews," said the Arabs; "now they want to get rid of their problem by pushing it off on us and using our land."

But the Arabs did not see Israel simply as a device of the West to rid itself of an unconscionable problem at the expense of another people. It was for them a tactic of fading imperial power to continue its control of Arab destinies. The position of the British in Arab lands was rapidly and irrevocably fading; now they sought to bolster up their weakness by creating Israel as a Western bridgehead, confronting the Arab world with a situation which would trouble and divide it. In the ensuing attack on the new state, the Arabs were not so much responding to the existence of Israel per se as to a long history of foreign control, domination, and manipulation at the hands of the great powers. Israel became, and has remained, the symbol of the Arab national struggle against foreign control.

This reaction was not merely a psychological fact of the Arab mind; it stemmed from and was given content by the process through which Israel came into being. The United Nations did not consult the wishes of the majority community in Palestine (the Arabs were nearly two thirds of the population) in regard to their political future. On the basis of Jewish ownership of some 23 per cent of the total cultivatable land area of the country, Israel was given nearly 40 per cent of Palestine. The vote in the United Nations which created the state came only after long debate and was due in part (the Arabs allege, with some justification) to the Western bloc and the pressure it was able to mount on client states. The Arabs have always maintained that the United Nations did not have the authority under its charter to dispose of their territory, especially without regard to the wishes of the inhabitants. They can only see that Israel was rammed down their throats by the same forces which so long had manipulated their national life.

Perhaps the Arabs should forget all this after nineteen years of fruitless struggle and recognize that history seldom moves to right past wrongs; but they have not, and they will not. After all, two decades is a short span in the thirteen centuries of Arab history; Palestine has been lost to the Arabs before and ultimately regained—it could happen again. The inherent superiority of Arab resources (presently thirty times the population of Israel and eight times its gross national product), the growing modernization of Arab life, the rising power of the non-Western world in international affairs, and the legitimacy of their aspirations make the Arabs feel that time is on their side more than it is on Israel's.

Moreover, the Arabs read Israel's policies since its founding as proof that it intends to be a law unto itself, not bound by the international community to which it owes its existence. On the eve of the creation of the new state, the Zionist radical underground launched a series of un-provoked attacks on certain Arab territories to force their inclusion within Israel, although they did not lie within the borders created by the United Nations resolution—a fact which has been acknowledged with some gratitude by Israeli leaders. In recent years, Israel has been deliberately un-cooperative with the United Nations Mixed Armistice Commission, refusing to participate in many of its meetings. After the 1956 attack on Egypt, Israel categorically refused the United Nations' request to station a new peacekeeping force (UNEF) on its soil, although Egypt accepted for its own territory in the Gaza Strip. The demilitarized zones, created by the Armistice Agreement which ended the 1948 fighting, have been a cause of continuing dispute. Repeatedly Israel has attempted to extend agriculture and land reclamation into these areas, over the Arab insistence that this violated their status quo under the agreement. This was one reason for the intermittent clashes along the Syrian border which led to the 1966-1967 Syrian hostility. In Arab eyes, this record gave the image of an aggressive Israel, only accepting United Nations controls and operations when they served its own purposes.

This image was sharpened by the one problem which, more than any other aspect of the existence of Israel, has stirred Arab resentment and fanned the embers of Arab hostility—the plight of the Arab refugee. As a result of the founding of Israel, over one million Arab inhabitants of

Palestine became refugees in neighboring countries. Nearly a quarter of the original refugee group fled their country before the British forces were withdrawn and Israel came into being. The remaining three quarters were uprooted during the hostilities and the period when the cease-fire was being negotiated. One of the first actions of the United Nations after the 1948 conflict was to call for the return of these refugees to their homes; on December 11, 1948, the General Assembly adopted a resolution stating "that refugees wishing to return to their homes and live at peace with their neighbors should be permitted to do so at the earliest practical date, and that compensation should be paid for the property of those choosing not to return and for the loss and damage to property."

This resolution was repeatedly reaffirmed, yet Israel did not take steps to implement it, the Israeli view being that it would discuss the refugee problem only in the context of a general peace settlement. The Arabs have maintained that the right of people to return to and reside on their own property is a basic human right, not subject to collateral conditions, and cite the UN resolution in defense of this.

Israel and some of its supporters have countered this claim by maintaining that the refugees left voluntarily, being lured from their homes by provocative Arab broadcasts which promised that they would return in triumph once victory had been won. There is no dependable historical evidence that this counterclaim was true; tapes allegedly recording such broadcasts have been cited, but never produced for impartial inspection. The fact is that most of the refugees fled because they were afraid, afraid of being caught between the lines of battle, afraid of terrorist raids by the Zionist underground such as that which destroyed the village of Deir Yassin on April 9, 1948, in which some 250 unarmed Arabs were massacred. Yet, regardless of the reasons for flight, the Arabs (and apparently the United Nations) have taken the view that a man has a right to return to his home no matter what the reason for his leaving—so long (as the UN resolution stated) as he intends to live peacefully with his neighbors.

This tragic situation has left in the heart of the Arab

world a mass of dislocated and bitter people, dependent on international charity for their existence, taxing the resources of the countries to which they have fled, and nursing a deep sense of grievance against those who now occupy their homes. Movements like the Palestine Liberation Organization and leaders like Ahmed Shukairy are not due so much to the calculated policy of Arab states as to the festering sore of the refugee camps. The failure of Israel to show any concern for this problem, to make any serious attempt to carry out the United Nations resolution, or even to admit a responsibility toward the refugees which it could not presently implement because of its own security problem is read by the Arabs as proof that Israel is basically anti-Arab.

Admittedly, these Arab views of Israel are partial, emotional, not taking into account Israel's own problems and the problem Israel itself was created to solve. The dispassionate political analyst will not read the situation either as the Arab or as the Israeli does. Both Arab and Israeli motives are mixed, and both highlight the factors which favor their cause and neglect those which weaken it. But Arab feelings are genuine, deep, founded upon a case which cannot be summarily dismissed as simply irrational hatred or political maneuver. This case and the feelings it engenders are a fundamental cause of the 1967 conflict; without taking full account of them, any explanation of Arab actions is partial and misleading.

It is still too early to establish a definitive account of all that transpired in precipitating the outbreak of hostilities in June, 1967, but there are certain general factors affecting the Arab action which are clear. One was the continuing effect on Egypt and the Arab world of the 1956 Israeli invasion of Egypt. Because this was followed by ten years of relative (if uneasy) calm, it has largely been forgotten in the West, but Egypt and President Nasser did not forget it. From that bitter experience, the military and political leadership of Egypt drew three conclusions.

The first was that Israel would "try it again" when a propitious opportunity for military action offered itself. In the winter and spring of 1967, the U.A.R. and Syria believed they had evidence that Israel might be preparing for another round. In response to continued border raids, Premier Eshkol gave public warning in the Knesset that Israel might take drastic action, hinting at a military retaliation against Syria. This warning was given unusual weight by the Syrians and Egyptians because of the Israeli punitive action against the Jordanian village of Es-Samu in November, 1966.

To Eshkol's warning was added the fact that at the annual parade in Jerusalem on Israel's Independence Day, some heavy military equipment was conspicuously absent—could it be massed on the borders of Syria for an attack? The suspicion was confirmed when the Soviets apparently reported to the Syrians in late April or early May that their intelligence had detected an Israeli armed concentration on the Syrian border. It is not possible to know whether this was a complete fabrication or rested upon some hard evidence; the important thing is that it confirmed Syrian and Egyptian fears. Shortly thereafter both the Syrian and Egyptian intelligence claimed that they had independent confirmation of the Soviet report.

Many will scoff at the idea that Israel was preparing to repeat its 1956 maneuver, or had any aggressive intent toward its neighboring Arab states. What is important is not the fact, but the belief in Syrian and Egyptian minds. Given the experience of a sudden Israeli attack eleven years earlier, which obviously had been well planned, it is not surprising that the Arabs were prepared to believe the worst. This belief did not concern Israel alone; it also included Arab estimates of Western policy. In 1956, Israel had been aided and abetted by France and Great Britain, the full story of whose complicity is just beginning to be revealed.

In 1967 it seemed to the Egyptians that Great Britain and the United States might be urging Israel on in its alleged aggressive policies. Britain and the U.A.R. had long been involved in a confrontation in South Arabia, where Egypt was supporting the most radical wing of the Aden national struggle. American-Egyptian relations had steadily deteriorated since 1965; American aid to the U.A.R. had virtually ceased, and by the winter of 1967 President Nasser believed that the United States had written off the U.A.R.

in its Arab policies and was determined to undermine his position. On several occasions he and other senior members of his government expressed the conviction that a "confrontation" between the two countries was inevitable. Given the American connection with Israel and the memory of the carefully concealed Anglo-French involvement in the 1956 affair, it seemed plausible that behind Israel's disquieting statements and (reported) military movements lay Anglo-American conniving.

A second lesson drawn from the 1956 experience was that never again could Egypt afford to be caught with its armed forces unmobilized in the face of a possible invasion. The 1956 attack caught the Egyptian Army completely unprepared—although the crescendo of border incidents should have warned them of the possibility of a major Israeli response. Defeated once by unpreparedness (as they saw it), they would not run the risk of a second experience. The development of the Egyptian Army after 1956, with its better training and larger supply of advanced weapons, gave confidence that if the army were in position, it could prevent an aggressive action, perhaps even carry war into Israeli territory. At the same time, mobilization would serve to warn Israel and those allegedly behind it that the U.A.R. was on to the game and would not be caught napping this time.

But in mobilizing, it is doubtful that the U.A.R. felt it ran too great a risk of actual conflict, for the third lesson it drew from 1956 was that the world community would not allow another war between Israel and the Arabs. President Nasser freely expressed this conviction on a number of occasions, saying that since the world community had stopped Israel in its attack against the Arabs in 1956, it would also stop an Arab attack against Israel, giving this as one reason why he opposed plans for a general Arab-Israeli war.

Despite the usual flood of bellicose statements, it does not appear on the basis of information now available that the U.A.R. was planning to attack Israel out of hand. It seems rather to have responded to what it considered the possibility of Israeli action by taking the step of complete and challenging mobilization on Israel's borders, believing that it could do so with safety on the basis of its own military strength and the probability that international forces would restrain Israel and find some way out of the situation short of war.

It may be argued that President Nasser's request for the withdrawal of UNEF from the Gaza Strip makes this view invalid, his true object being to get the United Nations out of the way so that he *could* attack Israel. No conclusive judgment can yet be given on this, but there is evidence which suggests that the U.A.R. did not expect or plan for the complete dismounting of the UN peacekeeping operation. From his standpoint, Secretary-General U Thant acted correctly; no UN peace force could remain on the soil of a host country over that country's objection. Moreover, it seems to have been the Secretary-General's conviction that unless a peacekeeping force had full freedom to exercise its function, it must be withdrawn, both to protect the UN from blame of ineffectiveness for which it was not responsible, and to secure freedom for future peacekeeping operations in other situations. Additionally, Yugoslavia and India appeared to be considering the withdrawal of their contingents from UNEF.

Despite these conditions and the logic they imposed on the situation, it appears that the U.A.R. was taken by surprise by the instant and complete dispersal of UNEF. Apparently President Nasser expected that the observers would be withdrawn from the borders to Gaza, then the matter carried back to the UN with delaying diplomatic tactics which might result in some compromise solution.

That this did not happen seems to have been an important element in the outbreak of conflict. Once the UNEF force was withdrawn from the Strait of Tiran, the Egyptian Army naturally replaced it. In Egyptian eyes this returned the Gulf of Aqaba to its pre-1956 position. The chief gain Israel had made from 1956 was the opening of the Gulf of Aqaba, which became the symbol to the Egyptians of their defeat and the unwarranted "fruit of aggression" on the part of Israel. The temptation was too strong to be resisted. Encouraged by plaudits from the Arab world, Nasser moved to erase the last blot from the Egyptian scutcheon and return his country's sovereignty over its own territory to what it had been before the Israeli attack in 1956.

In all this it is clear that the Egyptians were badly misled when they assumed that the world of 1967 was so like the world of 1956 that hostilities would be prevented by international action. American-Soviet cooperation was not possible, as it had been eleven years earlier. The Soviets were under pressure from their dispute with China and at odds with the United States over Vietnam. The problems of the NATO alliance, with the defection of France and the weakening of the British position, made united Western action highly improbable—as American failure to rally support against the closing of the Gulf of Aqaba showed. Israel had strengthened its political and foreign policy of self-determination and had increased its military power. 1967 was not 1956, and it was a calamitous miscalculation to assume that Arabs could confront Israel with impunity behind the shield of an expected international intervention.

While the memory of 1956 and the lessons the Arabs drew from it formed the general framework for their actions in 1967, there were at least two other important factors involved. The first was the relationship between the U.A.R. and Syria. After the dissolution of the Egyptian-Syrian union in 1961, the two countries entered a period of intermittent cold war and revolutionary rivalry. Syria has always felt that it was the wellspring of Arab unity, and its Baath Party was itself as the original and true delineator of Arab socialism. Nasser's claims to Arab leadership and socialist pioneering did not sit well with the Syrians, who resented what had happened to them under the United Arab Republic. Part of Syria's proprietary sense of Arab unity was expressed by its uncompromising stand against Israel; of all Arab countries, Syria was the most consistently provocative in its Israeli policies.

Syria was a problem to the U.A.R. Its stand against Israel could not be openly repudiated, nor its claim to revolutionary socialism written off. After some five years of tension, the U.A.R. moved (partly under Soviet prodding) to plaster over its differences with Syria, and in the fall of 1966, entered into a defensive alliance with Damascus. On the surface this appeared to be a move against Israel, but in fact it was partly a device through which the U.A.R. hoped to restrain Syrian adventures which might embroil the U.A.R. in an unplanned and undesired conflict. This objective was also present in the earlier formation of the Unified Military Command, a device by which the U.A.R. hoped to have some influence in the military planning of other Arab states as a partial guarantee against their unilateral action.

During the growing tension between Syria and Israel in the winter of 1967, the U.A.R. was relatively quiet, but after the major air battle in the early spring, when the Syrians were badly defeated, Syria pressed the U.A.R. to honor its commitment. Credibility is as important to the U.A.R. as it is to the United States, and Nasser either had to repudiate his undertaking or to fulfill it. Given the circumstance already described, and certain special Egyptian problems presently to be discussed, the U.A.R. threw in its lot with Syria, and to a measure, became a captive of that country's aggressive anti-Israel policies. That Nasser did this was due in part to his conviction that the U.A.R. military establishment could stand up against Israel should conflict break out.

This is only one illustration of how the Palestine problem has been a continuing factor in inter-Arab politics. This is the one issue on which no Arab leader can turn his back without risking his position, either in his own country or in the Arab world. Bourguiba was able to take a soft line toward Israel without imperiling his domestic position, but he paid for it by losing influence among his Arab neighbors.

This leads to the second factor in U.A.R. actions other than the impact of 1956—the particular problems Egypt was facing in its relations with the Arab world. After the Syrian defection in 1961 and President Nasser's growing stalemate in Yemen, Egyptian reputation steadily eroded. King Faisal's adroit diplomacy checkmated the U.A.R. on a number of occasions, the Unified Military Command, which Egypt had sponsored, began to break up,

110

divisions within the Arab League were so sharp that it was impossible to hold a proposed chief-of-states conference to consider common Arab problems. Thus the U.A.R. found itself increasingly isolated from many of its neighbors.

The issue went far beyond President Nasser's personal leadership. As the largest Arab state, Egyptian influence in recent years has been a constant and natural factor in Arab politics; no plans for concerted Arab action could be made without Egyptian concurrence and participation. As the possessor of the area's largest armed force, the center of revolutionary change, and the most active Arab state in international affairs, the U.A.R. could not be shoved aside without generating a sharp reaction.

This reaction did not create the recent Arab-Isreali clash as a cynical maneuver to regain lost influence. As has been made clear, the elements of the crisis were all present in the situation and in the Arab suspicions of Israel's intent. But as the crisis developed, it seems clear that the U.A.R. saw in it an opportunity to reassert its "natural" leadership and this in connection with the one issue which most unites the Arabs. If a clash with Israel seemed imminent, the U.A.R. could not stand aloof from it or afford (with its large military force) to be halfhearted in its involvement. This does not mean that Egypt decided to launch an overt and aggressive attack on Israel at the head of united Arab armies. There is good reason to believe that President Nasser was pursuing a political rather than a military objective, and believed that a determined stand against what he and the Arabs felt to be the threat of Israeli action might force the United Nations to review the situation and institute a settlement more favorable to the Arabs. This was a return to the 1948 situation rather than to 1956; what was sought was not simply to curtail possible Israeli invasion, but to reopen the entire question of Palestine, including the refugees, in the hope that some new UN resolutions might result.

It is not yet possible accurately to assess the degree and form of Soviet responsibility for Arab actions. Apparently the Egyptians did not consult or clear with the Soviets when they closed the Gulf of Aqaba, and the

Soviets did not support this action in their speeches at the Security Council. It has been claimed that Russian technicians participated in Syrian military action; if so, the number was small. There is no evidence that Russian personnel assisted the Egyptians.

It seems clear that the Soviets saw in the mounting tension between the Arabs and Israel an opportunity to increase their influence in the Arab world and to embarrass the United States while its attention was absorbed in Vietnam. In general, Soviet objectives have been served by keeping the Arab-Israeli dispute simmering, but not allowing it to come to a boil. To settle the conflict would increase the stability of the area, which the Soviets do not want; to push it to overt conflict would imperil their large investment in some Arab lands and risk the danger of a global confrontation.

Here the Russians seem to have miscalculated as badly as the Arabs. They apparently assumed that the United States could and would control Israel on the brink of conflict, throwing the matter into the United Nations, where they could wage a prolonged diplomatic campaign in support of the Arabs. Part of their miscalculation seems to have been based on unrealistic estimates of Arab strength, which, if it could not defeat Israel (as any competent Soviet military analyst must have known), could at least stand off an attack until international intervention carried the matter from the battlefield to the debates of the United Nations.

Had UN intervention developed, the U.A.R. would have had a political triumph which would have restored its waning leadership, set forward the unity of the Arab world, and alleviated some of the deep frustrations which the Arab-Israeli impasse had created. This was one reason why President Nasser was willing to play the game of brinkmanship in the Gulf of Aqaba and on the southern borders of Israel, setting the stage for an Israeli response while continuing to believe that the worst would not happen.

But the worst did happen; the Arabs miscalculated their own military strength, the ability of the international community to intervene, and the determination of Israel to use direct military measures. The stunning defeat which followed has made that clear beyond all doubt; what it has not made clear is that any of the basic forces involved in the Arab reaction to Israel's presence has changed or been obliterated. That is the problem of the future, and any course of action which assumes that the recent war has settled the long-term issue will be unrealistic and unproductive.

3.

UNITED STATES POLICY IN THE MIDDLE EAST

Dan Cordtz is a resident Washington Editor of "Fortune" magazine. Before joining "Fortune" in 1966, he was for 11 years a correspondent for "The Wall Street Journal," covering New York, Detroit, Paris and Washington.

116

BUT WHAT DO WE DO ABOUT THE ARABS?

Dan Cordtz

Two decades ago, in the eyes of nearly all Arabs, the U. S. towered over every other major power. Today America is a curse on the lips of many of the most intelligent and moderate in their ranks. "At this moment," claims an embittered Princeton-educated former Jordanian minister, "there is no Arab more extreme than the other. What I say about the U. S. is being said by every Kuwaiti, Saudi, or Libyan. Like Churchill, we are ready to make an alliance with the devil to keep ourselves alive." An American historian declares flatly that "not since the Boxer Rebellion has there been as rapid and ubiquitous a revulsion against a foreign power as there has been against the U. S. in the Middle East." And a man who once helped formulate our Arab policy sadly acknowledges that "our ability to play a role in that region has never been less than it is today."

This gloomy assessment is shared by many well-informed people in the U. S.—in government and outside. Some knowledgeable specialists in the State Department are very concerned about the precipitous decline in our influence.

117

So are the most respected academic experts on the Middle East and, when they are willing to discuss it, American businessmen with interests and long experience in the Arab lands. Their fears, together with the outrage and despair of Arabs who were once among America's closest friends, suggest the time has come for a realistic, full-scale reappraisal of our objectives in the Arab world, their priorities, and the means by which they can best be attained.

The stakes are great, and go far beyond our obvious interest in the safety of Israel. In a world of intercontinental ballistic missiles, the Middle East has lost some of its historic value as a strategic geographic area. Some, but not all. For the region is still the fastest, cheapest transportation route—by air or sea—between Western Europe and Asia. And still more important, beneath its desert sands lie close to 300 billion barrels of petroleum, about three-fourths of the non-Communist world's proved reserves. Daily production of the Arab wells totals more than nine million barrels. According to oil consultant Walter Levy, the complete loss of this oil could not be made up by any combination of other sources within a decade—if at all. Western Europe imports 5,600,000 barrels of Arab oil each day, 65 percent of its requirements, and Japan 1,200,000 (60 percent). If the Russians should achieve domination of the Arab countries, as many Arabs now fear they will, they could blackmail both Western Europe and Japan by threatening to turn off the taps and cripple their economies. The ultimate price for assured oil supplies, some American diplomats grimly speculate, could well be a sharp diminution of U.S. influence in Europe and Asia.

The major goal of most of our efforts in the Middle East is to keep that from happening. There are serious doubts today that we are succeeding. The Communist camel poked his nose under the tent in 1955 when Egyptian President Nasser, rebuffed by the U.S., turned to Czechoslovakia for weapons. In the years since, the beast has steadily made new encroachments. None of the Arab countries can yet be labeled Red satellites, but the Russian gains have been impressive and worrisome. In Syria, where a series of coups d'etat has wiped out layer on layer of educated leaders and many of those who remain are leftists, the army is Russian equipped and largely directed by Soviet advisers. Egypt, its economy almost bankrupt and its expensive military machine shattered, is more dependent than ever on Russian assistance. Two years after the elimination of Premier Ben Bella, Algeria still truculently proclaims its close friendship with Russia. And these are three of the weightiest Arab nations.

Underlying elements of strength remain to us: only recently escaped from colonial rule, the Arabs are not anxious to hand over their independence; even Nasser has kept local Communists under control and has moved quietly to restore communication with the U.S. And Communism, as an ideology, is incompatible with the Arabs' dominant Islamic faith. That said, though, re-emergence of the dormant Arab-Israeli conflict has so polarized Middle Eastern politics that there is danger that nearly all the Arab countries will ally themselves with the Soviet Union in opposition to Israel and its protector, the U.S. Anti-Communist Arabs frantically warn that this is already happening. According to a Lebanese statesman whose pro-Western credentials are beyond reproach, "The U.S. must ask itself this central question: 'Are we ready to hand over the Middle East to the Russians?' "

Measured against the U.S. Government's own formally enunciated goals, our present approach can hardly be termed a rousing success. We have failed to keep the Russians out or under control. We were unable to prevent an outbreak of hostilities. The Suez Canal is closed once more. Continued access to the oil, on acceptable terms, remains in doubt. It can even be argued that Israel's long-term security and prosperity, far from being enhanced, are today in greater jeopardy.

Some of these aims, it must be conceded, are so ambitious as to be almost unrealistic; perhaps no policy devised by human ingenuity can ever attain them all. Washington officials warn that "the first thing to remember is that we aren't God." One observes: "We found out in this latest Middle Eastern crisis that even we and the Soviets together couldn't give orders and expect people to snap their

119

heels and come to attention." There is much to this. The Arab world is not a "world" but a sprawling, diffuse collection of thirteen states with little in common but language. Our goals there are sometimes contradictory, as we seek to remain friendly with states antagonistic to one another. Our tools are limited: our military strength is unusable, our aid programs are hedged with restrictions demanded by Congress, and persuasion is often ineffective. In a sense, moreover, our efforts are subject to a double veto: Israel and its supporters can establish one boundary to our policy, and the oil-producing Arab states another.

The Loud, Persuasive Voice

The U.S. is actually confronted with two different though related sets of problems. The first, ever present in the background and at times totally overshadowing the other, arises out of our very special friendship with Israel. Virtually all the Arab countries' leaders came to power after Israel's establishment, and therefore began relations with the U.S. tacitly accepting our close ties with the Jewish state we had helped create. While the Middle East is quiet those ties can usually be ignored in the interests of cooperation. But when periodically the two sides clash, as they did over passage through the Gulf of Aqaba, U.S. support of Israel produces a poisonous Arab reaction.

The second group of complications have their origin in the frequently waspish relations among the Arab nations themselves. For a number of years this has really meant relations of each of the other nations with Nasser. Other regimes must come to grips with the Egyptian leader because he is, however much they may deplore it, the most popular political leader in the Arab world and the only Arab to whom *both* the big powers pay much attention. And he has evinced ambitions about his and Egypt's role in the Arab world that almost inevitably pose threats to leaders of the oil-producing lands, where our greatest material interests lie.

Nasser appears to be aiming for eventual unification of the Arab world under his domination. Part of his motivation is probably personal ambition. But he also seems to persuade millions that the welfare of Egypt and even the other Arabs will thereby be served. Wealth and population are unevenly distributed in the Middle East; Kuwait, Saudi Arabia, and Libya have lots of oil and few people, while Egypt is poor and crowded. Thus a combination, Nasser believes, would benefit everyone. And the region's political power, he reasons, would be enhanced if it spoke on the world stage with one voice. In his efforts, though, Nasser has run afoul of the nationalist aspirations of other Arab rulers, who are unwilling to submit to his leadership. While his appeal to the masses is great and extends to literally all of the Arab lands, he is regarded as a threat by many of their leaders—especially King Hussein of Jordon, King Faisal of Saudi Arabia, King Hassan of Morocco, and President Bourguiba of Tunisia.

In his drive to unify and lead the Arabs, Nasser has tried a number of different tactics. He joined with Syria and, later in 1958, Yemen, to form the United Arab Republic, then sadly watched its dissolution three years later after a Syrian Army revolt. He has been accused by other Arab chieftains of plotting to overthrow or assassinate them. He has employed Radio Cairo to pour out a steady stream of vilification on those who opposed him. He intervened in Yemen's civil war to gain a foothold in the Arabian Peninsula and to ensure a friendly regime in Aden when the British depart. More recently, of course, he used the tension of confrontation with Israel to force Hussein into a military pact. None of these stratagems has really been successful. From time to time, disappointed and chastened, Nasser retired behind his own borders vowing to concentrate on Egypt's internal economic problems. But an American acquaintance suggests that those problems are so staggering that Nasser can bear to look at them for only six months or so and then begins longing again for his old foreign adventures.

The official U.S. attitude toward Nasser has swung wildly from ardent cultivation to near-ostracism. A former government official who knows the Egyptian president well contends that we have always handled him exactly wrong— wooing him when we should have been firm and hitting

121

him too hard when the wooing didn't work. Thus in the early days of the Kennedy Administration, he suggests, we were overgenerous in granting aid to Egypt, then too precipitate in withdrawing it four years later when Nasser displeased us. Egyptian resentment was heightened by the fact that in the year before withdrawal 98 percent of the aid was food, which made it appear that we were condemning Egypt's poor to starvation out of spite.

There are those who believe, however, that we had lost any hope of getting along with Nasser long before that. They label the Israeli raid on the Gaza Strip in February, 1955, the beginning of the end. Nasser was appalled to discover, when the Israeli troops poured into Gaza, that they could just as easily have swept on to Cairo. He demanded that the U.S. sell him arms to counterbalance the Israeli strength. After months of unsuccessful haggling, he announced a deal with the Czechs for weapons in amounts and varieties far greater than anything he had asked from the U.S. In July, 1956, President Eisenhower's Secretary of State, John Foster Dulles, retaliated by backing down on commitments to help build the high dam at Aswan. A week later Nasser seized the Suez Canal, and three months after that Israel, Britain, and France invaded Egypt. Ultimately, of course, the U.S. played a major role in forcing the invaders out. But Dulles' legalistic rationalizations fanned little warmth in Egyptian breasts; some Egyptians blame us for bringing about the crisis in the first place.

In our dealings with other Arab countries, we have always been influenced by the thought of Nasser in the background. Thus we have quickly cooled to Arabs who seemed to share Nasser's radical aims: Syria, the Yemeni Republicans, sometimes Iraq. And we have been solicitous of those who appeared potential counterweights to Nasser. The most striking example, of course, is Jordan, where we have poured millions into an effort to create a viable economy in a state almost without resources. The weakness in this balancing policy has always been the Israeli question. When the Middle East is evenly divided between the revolutionaries and the conservatives, our material interests are reasonably protected. But where Israel is concerned, no

Arab leader is secure enough to stand by us while we maintain a posture of favoritism. It seems fair to ask if we might improve our prospects in the Arab world, and indirectly further Israel's best long-term interests, by a more visibly evenhanded approach.

A Commitment Abandoned

Evenhandedness, of course, is not always easy to attain. At times it is impossible. When Nasser announced the blockade of the Gulf of Aqaba, there was no middle ground. The U. S. had to accept it or oppose it; we opposed it. Similarly, when an intransigent Arab leader puts us in a position that challenges our commitment to Israel's existence, we have no room for maneuver. But there have been many examples of less inevitable partiality in the past that had already conditioned the Arabs to regard us as completely in the Israeli camp when trouble came. Official government aid to Israel ($1.1 billion), for example, almost equals that given Egypt over the past two decades—although Egypt has eleven times as many people. In that same period another $1 billion in private aid, by means of tax-deductible contributions to the United Jewish Appeal, has tipped the balance even more. And while the U. S. Government seldom hesitates to threaten the cutoff of aid when Arab regimes displease us, only at the time of the Suez invasion of 1956 did we use that stick on Israel. Much as we deplored the Israeli attack in June, we did not employ all the pressure available to us to head it off. After the cease-fire, moreover, the U. S. posture in the United Nations was plainly on the side of Israel. However compelling our reasons, we abandoned an unconditional seventeen-year-old commitment —reaffirmed as recently as May 23 by President Johnson— to the territorial integrity of all the states in the Middle East. We also abstained on the Pakistani resolution deploring Israel's take-over of Jerusalem, although we had publicly criticized such action. Not surprisingly, even the more moderate Arabs were outraged.

Some studies of what can be done to restore our badly damaged position are under way in the government, but there is reason to doubt that they are as searching and critical as the situation may require. Early in the crisis, President Johnson appointed a special task force run by former White House aide McGeorge Bundy, giving the impression that Washington was taking a hard new look at our policies. But Bundy has now gone back to his duties at the Ford Foundation and is spending only part time on the Washington project. Officials are at pains, moreover, to deny that any criticism of the past was implied by the task force's appointment. It was designed merely to help coordinate operations related to Middle Eastern problems, they explain.

"Opinion is a Very Flexible Thing"

The fact is that Washington policy makers, while they insist they are not complacent, seem remarkably unalarmed. Consoled by what they call disastrous Soviet losses, they discount the view of moderate Arabs that our own losses have been even more severe. They appear to regard Arab emotions as not truly a factor in the equation, or at least as too unreliable to consider in planning future action. Some speak confidently, and even condescendingly, of how fickle those emotions are. ("Opinion is a very flexible thing in the Arab world," a responsible official remarks. "An Egyptian journalist once told me that it takes three days to change public opinion in Egypt.") They count heavily on the traditional divisions of the Arab world and fear of Communism to send some of its leaders scurrying back to us for aid and protection.

They also recognize the formidable built-in political resistance to any consideration of new directions in American Middle Eastern policies. The overwhelming majority of U. S. citizens neither know nor care anything about the region. Most of those who do care are emotionally partial to Israel, and many of these are effectively vocal in their support. Few of the remainder can or will make themselves heard. Either they are dissuaded by fears of being labeled anti-Semitic, or their small voices are lost in the void of public indifference.

This near-unanimous backing for Israel handicaps U. S. diplomats in the Arab world. In the recent fighting, cer-

tainly, Israel benefited from the fact that the Syrians and
Egyptians had provoked the crisis and had made noisy
threats about their intentions. But the American public's
sympathy for Israel has been obvious throughout the little
country's history. "There's nothing we can do about that
partiality," says a former U.S. ambassador to a major
Arab capital. "It's the great embarrassment of the official
policy in the Middle East."

The one-sided attitude of the American public, moreover, reflects more than their sympathetic feelings about
the Israelis. Americans react negatively to their image of
the Arabs as backward, cruel, largely uncivilized desert
dwellers—an image, according to one Arab scholar, derived
from dimly recalled, badly taught Sunday-school stories and
unconscious religious hostility toward Islam. There is no
real knowledge to counter the myths. Certainly there is
little awareness of the Arabs' illustrious history, a fact that
infuriates them. And far too often the Arabs, as some of
them admit, have been their own worst enemies. Many of
their leaders have offended U.S. voters and their representatives. Extravagant language is much admired in the Arab
world, for example, but Americans tend to take it at face
value.

On the other hand, we have made no effort whatever to
look at the problems of the Middle East through Arab
eyes. To do so is to begin to discern the dimensions of
their grievances. There are many—not all of them entirely
realistic. Many Arabs believe we want them militarily weak
and divided, which may well be true so long as Nasser
remains the obvious candidate to lead a united Arab world.
They suspect we want to retain, through our aid programs
and other means, much of the influence of the old colonial
powers. They charge that we have brought them into the
cold war by forcing Egypt to turn to the Communists for
weapons and by labeling neutrality immoral. They complain
that our assistance to them is niggardly and motivated not
by friendship but by self-interest. These grievances have long
existed, but they have been given special force by dramati-
zation of the more serious Arab charge that we are blatantly
partial where Israel is concerned. So strongly do they feel

125

about this that many who reject Nasser's charges of direct U.S. involvement in the war regard our financial and diplomatic support of Israel as almost equally reprehensible.

The Irreplaceable Oil

Only the complaint about Israel is universal. But it has inflamed even basically pro-Western Arabs so much that many are now inclined to endorse the other accusations as well. And the compulsion to strike back jeopardizes, to a greater degree than ever before, our stake in the Arab countries' oil. There is considerable reluctance, on the part of American oilmen no less than government officials, to make much of this stake in public. They realize that it is all but impossible, in a nation with the popular traditions of the U.S., to suggest that material interests should be weighed along with such human considerations as Israel's welfare. It is senseless, however, not to face up to the very real possibility of the loss of the oil and the implications of such a loss.

In ten years, development of alternative sources of energy could reduce Arab oil's importance drastically. But for now it is quite literally irreplaceable. Even the present partial boycott has created serious hardships for Britain. The added transportation costs and higher prices for substitute oil amount to roughly $1 million a day. The U.S., whose Arab petroleum imports amounted to only 350,000 barrels a day, has not suffered, but individual American companies have been hurt. As a group, U.S. oil firms have a gross investment of nearly $3 billion ($1.5 billion net after depreciation) in the Arab lands, and their profits from production there last year amounted to more than $1 billion.

It is by no means clear what the oil companies' fate will be. The largest Arab oil-producing states, thus far, have not shown great enthusiasm for the total shutdown advocated by some Arab countries. The measures they have taken, in fact, were the least they could do as members of the Arab world. But oilmen still have their fingers crossed. An unhappy executive in Beirut says, "It would be difficult for me to lay a bet on our being here five years from now, and if we are the situation won't be easy."

Yet immediate nationalization of the fields and expulsion of the foreign operating companies is unlikely. The idea has long appealed to many Arab leaders, including some whom the U.S. Government regards as friends. Even splitting the proceeds about sixty-forty with the companies, and selling at the lowest prices in the world ($1.59 per barrel for Kuwaiti oil compared with $2.27 for Venezuelan crude), the oil-producing countries take in an estimated $2.5 billion a year in royalties and taxes from the oil firms. If they could keep all the selling price, and could agree among themselves to raise that price, the wealth generated —for economic development or weapons—would be staggering. Nationalization, however, would be far from easy to carry out. Arab experts agree that all the countries would have to take the step together and this just doesn't seem to be in the cards under the present circumstances.

Even if the countries could coordinate nationalization, they would face the formidable problem of selling their oil. The marketing outlets in the major oil-consuming regions are in private hands. Unless the evicted companies agreed to buy the oil, foregoing their share of the most profitable phase of the business, the Arabs would have almost no place to turn. "It would be very difficult to replace the financial resources of the Western world," admits an Arab petroleum expert.

If nationalization is only a remote threat, however, some form of painful squeeze on the companies is probable. A continuation of the crisis, in fact, seems likely to bring unwelcome changes in the structure of the industry. The French are vigorously seeking to convert President de Gaulle's stance into material advantage by improving their position in the Arab oil fields. And the Italian Government oil agency, E.N.I., which has long coveted access to Arab oil, now seems within sight of its goal. Talks between E.N.I. and the Iraqi Government have been going on since 1961, when Iraq announced the expropriation of about 99 percent of the Western consortium's acreage. Now the Italian Government reportedly is dangling a $70-million low-interest loan in exchange for a development contract for E.N.I. American oilmen are resigned to seeing both the French and the Italians achieve some measure of success.

It appears certain that the companies will have to settle for a smaller share of the oil revenues. Three weeks after the cease-fire, Bierut's authoritative *Middle East Economic Survey* noted that "Arab oil producing countries, to fulfill their role as financiers of the Arab world, will have to insure a steady increase in their oil revenues, not only in terms of over-all payments but also in terms of per-barrel payments." Even if the situation quiets down, therefore, the outlook is for slimmer profits and more painful headaches in the oil business. And if large-scale fighting should break out once more, with the U.S. sympathetic to the Israelis, expulsion of American firms would be a real possibility, no matter how self-destructive that might be.

What's Good for Israel?

In spite of its importance, if our interest in the oil conflicted directly with our concern for Israel, we would probably regretfully have to watch the oil go down the drain. But our stake in both may well call for some shift in our position. A good case can be made that Israel, for reasons easy to understand, has been pursuing a course that is not in its own best long-term interests. It can further be argued that the U.S. has encouraged these unwise policies by failure to view the Middle East from a more dispassionate and balanced position. Thus the U.S. alienated the Arabs and was unable to dissuade Israel from action that may have made its existence all the more precarious. The shock waves from Israel's victory are still sweeping across the Middle East. Ironically, U.S. officials say, they threaten most damage in the very lands that had been most tolerant toward Israel. The tiny Jewish state's long-range security, moreover, may not truly be enhanced by boundary changes or declarations of an end to belligerency or even free passage through the Gulf of Aqaba. Ultimately, Israel can prosper only if its Arab neighbors can be reconciled to its presence.

In the long sweep of history the Arabs have a lot going for them. The Western world tends to view Israel even now as the underdog—a tiny Jewish David facing the Arab Goliath. This is true in terms of total populations (2,500,000 Israelis versus 110 million Arabs) and geographic area, but today the Israelis are almost a match for the Arabs in terms of citizens able to play a constructive role in modern society—those in good health, educated, skilled, and possessed of high morale. The Arabs are not likely to remain forever industrially backward, unable to employ the tools of destruction effectively. In spite of many mistakes and setbacks, a remarkable amount of progress has already been made in education in the past decade. By 1990, moreover, the Arabs are expected to number more than 200 million to Israel's six million, at present rates of growth. If the tensions cannot be eased somehow, Israel one day *will* face overwhelming force. Even protected by nuclear weapons or foreign allies, it will then only be able to emulate Samson and destroy its enemies along with itself.

In spite of this prospect, there has been almost no progress toward defusing the explosive animosity. Israeli policy seems directed above all at forcing the Arabs formally to admit defeat and, by implication, to accept as settled many issues still outstanding. But viewed in long-range terms, this reverses the logical order of events. First, the issues that divide the antagonists should be resolved; then a formal end to hostilities could follow almost as a matter of course. Arab leaders now find it impossible to acknowledge Israel under duress. And even if they can be forced to do so, their signatures on a peace treaty will never prevent further warfare while the basic causes of Arab hostility remain. After almost two decades of no progress toward reconciliation, Israelis and their American well-wishers should examine soberly the possibility that a change of strategy could bring better results.

A Possible New Approach

It is obviously far easier to criticize past policies than to formulate new ones. There are no dramatic new initiatives to propose, and no one can say with assurance that this or that program will work. But what might offer some hope is a new *approach,* one that focuses not on securing contro-

129

versial and possibly unessential Israeli "rights" but on helping the Arabs regain their self-respect. Over the long run,
this can be done only by the Arab countries themselves,
by means of development that enables them to view themselves as the economic and political equals of Israel. For
the shorter term, however, there are at least two offenses
to Arab pride that could be eliminated: the unhealed sore
of the refugees from 1948 violence and the presence on Arab
soil of conquering Israeli soldiers. By persuading the Israelis to take a generous attitude on these two issues, moreover, the U.S. could demonstrate its impartiality in a way
that would strengthen the hand of its own embarrassed
Arab friends—e.g., Hussein of Jordan, Faisal of Saudi
Arabia, *et al.*

The form and dimensions of the refugee problem may
have been altered substantially by the outcome of the fighting. The Israeli forces overran, and now, occupy, territory
where about half of the refugees lived before the war
started. It is impossible to predict how many will end up
in Israeli-occupied territory. An undetermined number fled
to areas still in Arab hands and, although Israel has agreed
to permit some of them to return, it is still unclear how
liberal the Israeli Government will be about their repatriation. But it is certain that Israel has under its jurisdiction
a large share of the refugees.

There has been speculation that Israel will now move to
integrate them into the economic life of the captured lands.
In this there may be some wishful thinking. For the west-
bank region of Jordan, although already developed to a
considerable degree, was crowded before its occupation. It
may be impossible to absorb all of the refugees there, and
thus far Tel Aviv has shown no willingness to take them
back into pre-war Israel. Signs of Arab resistance to Israeli
rule in Old Jerusalem, moreover, cast doubt on the assumption that many Arabs will live willingly under the government of Israel. It is conceivable that events may prove to
have diminished the refugee problem. On the other hand, it
may turn out that the situation has only been complicated
further. Certainly the way in which the Israeli-controlled
refugees are treated could play a part in determining the

future attitude of reasonable Arabs. And the U.S., by insisting on fair and considerate treatment, could help regain its position among these Arabs.

The "Old" Refugee Problem

But there still remains the "old" refugee issue, which has been nagging the conscience of the world since 700,000 refugees fled Palestine when Israel was established. In nineteen years their numbers have swollen to 1,300,000 and they lived, before the latest fighting broke out, in Lebanon, Syria, Jordan, and the Gaza Strip. Some exist in the worst squalor; the luckiest occupy monotonous, crowded, but relatively livable camps operated by the United Nations Relief and Works Agency. Even they are housed, clothed, fed, and inadequately educated on a daily allowance of 10 cents per person.

The U.S. contributes the lion's share toward their subsistence; it has given $403 million of the $599 million donated to refugee care through last year. Private citizens recently formed a Near East Emergency Donations Committee (NEED) to channel additional corporate and individual donations to the agency in the current emergency. Periodically, U.S. officials have attempted to promote a settlement. Invariably, rebuffs from one side or the other have made us throw up our hands. Israel has attempted to use the refugees as bargaining counters in its campaign to force Arab recognition. The Arabs have seen them as their strongest claim on the decency of the West—their only good card in the propaganda game.

Israel has much to gain from elimination of the problem. Besides being pitiable, the refugees are extremely dangerous. From their ranks have come most of the commando-type raiders who periodically cross into Israel and stage terrorist attacks. It is their presence, as an organized, easily manipulated pressure group, that has kept Arabs of good will at the mercy of lowest-common-denominator politics. If, as Arab extremists suggest, Israel is to be turned into "another Vietnam," it will be refugees who provide the guerrillas.

Working out a detailed plan will be difficult, the more so as such a plan may well face Arab attempts to sabotage it by pressure on the refugees. But it surely is not beyond human capability. Its provisions will presumably have to include acceptance by Israel of a sizable portion of the refugees as repatriates (although this requirement could perhaps be satisfied by continued occupancy of Israeli territory by the refugees now there), generous compensation for the others, invitations to many to resettle in the U. S. and other countries, and intensive training designed to make them attractive as human resources throughout the Arab world. If the plan is generous enough, and reasonable enough, it will be extremely difficult for the most intransigent Arab leader to refuse it, standing up indefinitely to the combined pressure of world opinion, his own citizens, and the refugees themselves.

In the excitement of Israel's overwhelming military success, it may be easier to persuade the Israelis to tackle the refugee problem than to give up the leverage of their territorial gains. But it might be well for the U. S. to encourage them to consider withdrawal—and without some of the prior conditions on which they now insist. It is by no means obvious that the terms sought by Israel will really contribute to the future peace of the area and hence to its own ultimate interests. Such a withdrawal might seem a return to the conditions that brought on the fighting, and a pointless abandonment of hard-won fortified defense positions. But it could be argued that the Arab fortifications on the Syrian heights and the massed troops in the Sinai Desert were symptoms, not causes, of the hostility. Arab resentment of Israel's presence—the basic cause of the fighting—has been intensified by Israeli occupation of Arab territory. Some diplomats believe that from its present position of strength, Israel could well afford to hand back some of the land, undercutting Arab charges that it is aggressive and expansionist.

U. S. officials argue that it is too early to expect the Israelis to mitigate their conditions. Internal political considerations make it difficult for Prime Minister Eshkol to do so at the moment. In 1956, American diplomats point out, even under the combined pressure of the U. S. and the Russians, Israeli troops remained four months in the

Gaza Strip and at the mouth of the Gulf of Aqaba before withdrawing. Publicly, however, we have given no indication that we wish to see the Israelis withdraw—except on their own original terms, which American officials concede would be dangerous for any Arab leader to accept. And if we have been active behind the scenes, no effects are visible.

Regional Economic Development

If, by whatever means, the immediate crisis can be damped down and the attention of the Arabs directed away from revenge, the prospects for eventual development of the region are good. The impact of the war has, at least temporarily, revived the goal of unified effort and shown Arab leaders how badly they need to strengthen themselves. If ever a section of the globe cried out for regional development, it is the Middle East. Of the oil-rich countries, only Iraq has the resources to become a balanced agricultural-industrial state. Kuwait, Saudi Arabia, Abu Dhabi, and Libya combined have about ten million residents, and almost all their land is desert. Yet their oil resources generate tremendous amounts of capital, most of which cannot be constructively employed within their own borders. So great are the returns from oil that the Middle East, given technical assistance and encouragement, could probably finance its own development with almost no foreign financial aid.

Kuwait has for six years shared some of its great oil wealth by way of loans and bank deposits totaling nearly $700 million. Some expanded version of the Kuwait Fund for Arab Economic Development, with other oil-producing countries joining in support, is probably the most promising vehicle for development. Dr. Talha Yaffi, economist and general manager of Kuwait Investment Co., has worked out in some detail how such an inter-Arab fund could be financed and the large sums of money that it could provide for development. Under his proposal, all oil-producing countries would be obliged to contribute 5 per cent of their oil revenues, to be matched by an equal contribution by the private foreign companies holding the oil concessions. If the organization were started this year on that principle, he says, it would immediately have $308 million at its disposal.

133

By 1990, he estimates, it would have taken in $14 billion. Such amounts dwarf the $3.8 billion in American economic and military aid to the Arab countries over the last decade.

Consideration is also once more being given to the establishment of a Middle Eastern Development Bank. From the standpoint of the U.S., this would offer an opportunity to play a direct role in development of the region. Involvement in such a scheme at this time might be difficult to sell Congress, because it could commit the U.S. to large-scale support of programs devised in considerable degree by others. But it would help convince the Arabs that we are not determined to force an American solution to Middle Eastern economic problems.

Irrigation and Electricity

Spending all the funds wisely, of course, would be anything but automatic. Planners and developers can be hired, however, and patterns have already been set elsewhere. A notable example is the integrated regional-development program being carried out in Iran's Khuzestan province by the Development & Resources Corp. of New York. Formed in 1955 by David Lilienthal and Gordon Clapp, two former Tennessee Valley Authority chairmen, the company has reclaimed 50,000 acres from the desert and plans eventually to turn an additional 200,000 acres into productive agricultural land. Farm output in the province has already increased two and a half times as a result of the large-scale irrigation and hydroelectric-dam systems. Development & Resources is carrying out fourteen other projects around the world, and its officials are more than willing to take on part of an Arab development program.

A dramatic possibility for development is the plan devised by Rear Admiral Lewis Strauss, former chairman of the Atomic Energy Commission, and strongly supported by former President Eisenhower. It calls for the construction of three huge nuclear-powered plants to produce electricity and to convert seawater into fresh water. The water would then be used to irrigate thousands of acres of land that is now desert. Strauss estimates the cost of the project at around

$1 billion and has proposed that the U.S. put up half of the initial $200-million capitalization.

By any standard, the U.S. has a huge stake in the tranquility of the Middle East. As a high-ranking State Department official puts it: "We can't have another one of these wars every few years. It's too costly and it's too damned dangerous." Among other things, this is probably the last war the Arabs and Israel can fight without employing fearfully destructive and sophisticated weapons. The escalation from 1956 is itself sobering.

The obstacles that confront the U.S. in its efforts to play a constructive role are admittedly greater than at any time since it moved onto the Middle Eastern stage, and it will take time to restore our exhausted credit with the Arabs. But the effort must be made. Our own safety is too intimately involved to write off the Arabs. And if we are not to write them off, our policy makers may well have to move visibly into a posture of more balanced friendship with both sides. The war, and our pro-Israeli stance, have cut the ground from beneath those Arabs who were our advocates. If they are to take a public position favorable to us again, we must give them something to rally around. It is equally true that the Arabs will have to respond positively. Our commitment to Israel's existence is not negotiable.

From our own point of view, the beginning of wisdom is to understand that we are in serious trouble in the Arab lands, and that we cannot just wait patiently for them to get over their anger. If we make no moves, our adversaries could win the game by default.

Elmer Berger, a founder of the American Council for Judaism in 1943, has been its Executive Vice President since 1955. He has traveled extensively through the Middle East—in the Arab countries and the state of Israel—and is unusually well informed on the complex issues in that troubled area. A "moderate" in his approach to Middle East problems, Rabbi Berger has specialized in issues relating to the Zionist controversy and the preservation of American Judaism as a religion of universal values. He is the author of "The Jewish Dilemma," "A Partisan History of Judaism," "Judaism or Jewish Nationalism" and scores of articles.

This article was originally delivered at the Southeastern Massachusetts Technological Institute on November 15, 1967.

136

PROBLEMS OF AMERICAN POLICY MAKERS IN THE MIDDLE EAST

Elmer Berger

There is no problem in whole spectrum of American foreign policy in which it is more hazardous to challenge the consensus than the problem of our country's relations with the Middle East. This is particularly true if the context of consideration is Arab-Israeli-U. S. relations.

This is no new hazard. Its genesis lies in what might be called the conflict of politics and policy. Two decades ago, in the frenzied politics of the 1947-48 campaign, James Forrestal, then our first Secretary of Defense, cautioned eloquently about the distortions of American national interests in the Middle East due to domestic political pressure on the major parties. At one point, he recorded in his diaries that he had told the Secretary of State, James Byrnes:

> . . . I thought it was a most disastrous and regrettable fact that the foreign policy of this country was determined by the contributions a particular bloc of special interests might make to the party funds.[1]

In 1958, Dr. George Lenczowski wrote:

> These twists in American policy were to a large extent due to the division of responsiblity between the White

137

House and the Department of State. While the latter was concerned with the Middle East as a whole, the former tended to treat the Zionist problem in isolation from the rest of the area and as a factor of domestic politics; hence, the inconsistencies. The White House prevailed on all important occasions, and despite its tortuous ways American diplomacy could generally be described as pro-Israeli.[2]

For more recent examination of these pressures—and a detailed exposure of how they are brought about in American life—there are 300 pages of testimony given under oath in 1963 to the Committee on Foreign Relations of the U.S. Senate.[3] This testimony makes fascinating reading. Here, among other things, we learn that 5 million dollars were spent over a period of about seven years in activities which can be described only as those of unregistered foreign agents.[4] Furthermore, a substantial part of this not insignificant amount of money came from tax-deductible contributions to the United Jewish Appeal. Much of this money, given innocently enough in response to charitable appeals in behalf of distress immigration to Israel, found its way back to the United States through what Senator Fulbright called "conduits," to support Israeli press services, to subsidize chairs at distinguished American universities, to finance trips to Israel for news media people and other potential propaganda voices. Naturally this has all been designed to further the Israeli cause.

This situation has shaped the almost unchallenged assumption that what is good for Israel is good for the United States; and the further assumption that staunch support of Zionism is not incompatible with responsible American citizenship.

It is only candid to admit that the statement I have just made is slanted, implying that something other than the best interests of the United States is at the heart and core of Zionism and Israeli propaganda. It must be clear, therefore, that in a democracy where enlightened public opinion is essential for the formulation and implementation of a rational foreign policy, one of the first problems confronting American policy makers in dealing objectively with the Middle East is

138

this long history of formidable pro-Zionist and pro-Israel propaganda.

In the determination of a national policy, all assumptions need challenging. To determine whether what is good for Israel is, in fact, good for the United States—it is essential to define the United States' interests in the Middle East as a whole and, further, to examine strategies and tactics acceptable to the United States to defend and, perhaps, advance those interests. I will list here what I consider to be four basic interests which cover United States' converns in the area.

First, as an overall objective, there is the containment of the spread of Communist power in the area. An important corollary to this policy objective is to realize it without major military confrontation between the super-powers. I do not believe that "anti-Communism" is an adequate rationale for American foreign policy. There must be substantive interests, vital to our national life and outstanding on their own merit. The three other reasons for United States' concern fall into this category.

Two of these have been put briefly and well in an excellent article by Dan Cordtz, which appeared in *Fortune* magazine for September 1, 1967. The article is significantly entitled, "But What Do We Do About the Arabs?" The author begins with an analysis of the United States interests in the area and then he succinctly states the next two specific reasons for our concern:

> . . . the region is still the fastest, cheapest transportation route—by air or sea—between Western Europe and Asia. And still more important, beneath its desert sands lie close to 300 billion barrels of petroleum, about three-fourths of the non-Communist world's proved reserves. . . .[5]

Finally, the Middle East is comprised of developing nations. As such, they command our interest and concern for a vital aspect of American foreign policy is the desire for the orderly evolution of these former subjects of colonialism into stable, peaceful societies.

These four considerations should provide the framework within which American policy makers look at the Middle

East. It takes no more than a casual glance to realize the fact that not one of these vital interests and important strategic considerations lies *within* the State of Israel, is dependent on the State of Israel, or ultimately could be safeguarded by the State of Israel. Despite this fact, our policy posture in the entire area is now conditioned by commitment to support of the national sovereignty of Israel. This commitment began officially with support of the Palestine partition plan in 1947 and subsequent recognition of Israel as a nation-state. It may be that this commitment was imprudent if viewed in terms of long-range American interests. There can be little question that both Western and Soviet support for Zionist territorial claims in 1947 flouted basic democratic principles and ignored fundamental human rights insofar as the Arabs were concerned.

To the point of constituting a threat to our national interests this commitment jeopardizes our relations with the majority of people inhabiting the area from Casablanca to the Persian Gulf and sometimes reverberating even into Pakistan, India, and the heavily Muslim parts of Africa. And because this is true and because Zionist drumbeating propaganda is dedicated to maintaining this preferential relationship, the Zionist apparatus operated in the United States by the Israeli government is a major—perhaps the major—obstacle in the way of policy makers seeking to establish a rational American policy in the area.

That some policy makers are plainly aware of this inhibiting problem is clearly evidenced by a blunt statement of Senator Fulbright commenting on the question of Senate action with respect to freedom of transit for Israeli shipping through the Suez Canal. On April 28, 1960, Fulbright told the Senate:

> I hope no one in the Senate is so naive as to believe that the amendment will accomplish its ostensible purpose which is to open the Suez Canal to Israeli shipping and to end the Arab economic boycott against Israel. What it will accomplish is to annoy the Arabs and fortify them in their conviction that in any issue arising from the Arab-Israeli controversy the United States, because of domestic political pressures, will be on the

side of the Israelis. This Arab conviction for which I regret to say history affords some justification, is the greatest single burden which American diplomacy has to carry in the Middle East.[6]

It would appear so far that in my opinion the problems of our relations with the area stem from our support of the state of Israel. This is not entirely true, yet I hastily add that our tactics in dealing with the problems which are indigenous to the area are directly affected by our support of Israel. Of this there can be no doubt or question. At the same time, it would be less than honest to say that in the Middle East—as in all areas of the world where there are emerging nations, impoverished and less than literate people— there are no problems which are truly indigenous. These problems, however, should be scrutinized by the American policy maker and judged on their own merits, not in terms of any other context. Our integrity as a nation demands this.

It would be fruitless to attempt here to give a catalogue of the indigenous problems of the area. Our primary concern must be with those which have global implications. Suffice it to say, therefore, that there are at present three incipient wars, or conditions of intense hostility in the Middle East which concern the rest of the world. Each of these confronts American policy makers with a problem. All three of these conflicts are interrelated and our attitude toward any one of them affects our approach to all the others.

First, there are the Soviet and, to a lesser extent, the Chinese Communist aspirations for control of the area. These aspirations and the steps that have been recently taken to achieve them have converted the Middle East into an arena of the "Cold War." In this, the Soviets would appear to have gained an advantage for whether they like it or not, the majority of Arab countries are now dependent upon the USSR for support in their struggle with Israel. This situation is not without irony for the Soviets made the partition of Palestine possible and were among the first to provide the new state of Israel with arms and military material—channeled through a Communist satellite, Czechoslovakia— in 1948-49.

The second category of internal Middle East problems

which confronts our policy makers revolves about internecine quarrels among the various Arab states themselves. The history of Arab unity is, indeed, largely one of failure to find workable and pragmatic structures which would institutionalize deep-seated Arab emotion and motivation on a functional basis. There are many reasons for these failures. Among them are the character of the Arabs themselves, interference from outside the area, fairly recent escape from colonial control—all coupled with an eager desire to rush headlong into a still elusive future. Whether Arab unity is an aspiration which draws its strength from a romanticized history or is merely an example of Arab eloquence is a debate which consumes the attention of academicians and students of the area. But be that as it may, no policy maker can expect to make any headway in genuine, stable, and meaningful relations with the Arab world by frontal attack on the concept or by conduct which wholly ignores the phenomenon.

In the Arab world, there is a full 180 degree spectrum of governmental institutions and societal structures. At one end are the isolated and almost medieval absolutists of the sheikdoms on the Persian Gulf. There is the conservative royalty of Saudi Arabia, and Nasser of Egypt, the zealous crusader for what is called Arab Socialism. Somewhere between these stands the sophisticated, commerce-minded parliamentary system of Lebanon, the precariously balanced and for some time now the stultified revolution of Iraq, the Ba'athist regime in Syria, and the moderate, enlightened monarch in Jordan. On the African continent, there is the monarchy in Morocco, the tempestuous regime in Algeria, the individualistic, quietly progressive government of Bourghiba in Tunisia; there is the monarchy in Libya which struggles with all the ramifications of newly developed wealth and which for the time being depends on aging King Idris for stability. To these must be added the Sudan; belonging to both Black Africa and the Arabs, it suffers the agonies of both.

Confronted with the varied traditions, governments, and cultures of the Arab world, the American press more often than not calls it "turmoil" and with singular irresponsibility relates it to alleged instabilities in "the Arab character." Nothing could be really further from the truth. That which the press would call turmoil is in fact the seething cauldron of hope and aspiration of a people who are caught up in what is perhaps our era's most compelling phenomenon—"the revolution of rising expectations," as Adlai Stevenson so aptly described it. The superficiality of the American press—and of other communications media—does not alter the substance of the problem. It does not mitigate the rising self-consciousness of these people. It discourages but does not defeat the struggling Arab intellectuals. It frustrates, sometimes, but does not obviate the passion for social improvement which is sometimes so compelling that it results in less than carefully thought-out plans and in extravagant experiments. Of this, the American press is critical. But it ill behooves us, standing within the glass house of our domestic and foreign policy, to throw stones at those who dream of nationhood!

Moving from the political to the economic, it must be noted here that the largest American capital investments are to be found in the Arab states where progress is more cautious. There is a large measure of truth in the allegations that Gamal Abdel Nasser has been—and probably still is—the symbol of revolution to the masses in the conservative centers of American interests. But it is an over-simplification to credit all of the popular unrest in the Arab world to a super-powerful Cairo influence as is so often done by some American policy makers, and by some citadels of information in the United States, especially the *New York Times.* The more realistic analysis is that Nasser is the kind of charismatic figure throughout the Arab world which Winston Churchill, Franklin Roosevelt, or John Kennedy were on the broader stage of history. Only the charisma of such a leader is responsible for one finding his photograph in the lowliest peasant homes in Iraq, Lebanon, or even in Jordan. I am afraid that American policy makers have not always read this fundamental situation accurately. They have alternately wooed and then spurned Nasser—and therefore the Egyptian people, and therefore the most populous of the Arab states—hoping either to contain his influence in the Arab world which is equated with revolution, or to ride its tide to fulfillment. When they have spurned the Egyptian, they have—too often and too clumsily—embraced one of the seemingly promising alternatives to Nasser on the conservative side. And, most catastrophic of all, at times this embrace of alternatives to Nasser's prestige has zeroed in on Israel.

By playing off the revolutionaries with the conservatives, American policy has now proceeded to fuse the problem of internecine Arab differences into the broader conflicts of the "cold war." Since February of 1955, when Nasser turned to the West for arms after the first big Israeli raid into Gaza and the West refused—or set conditions which amounted to a virtual refusal—the Soviets eagerly seized the opportunity. As a result, today they are the major supplier of arms to the majority of Middle Eastern states.

The dilemma for the United States, the West and the liberal, often Western-oriented Arab intellectual or statesman, is not a happy one.

Central to all the problems which the Middle East presents to American policy makers is the Arab-Israeli conflict. One of the reasons why there has been so little progress toward resolution of this problem is the tendency to approach it one-dimensionally. This conflict cannot be resolved in any context favorable to American interests if it is not viewed against the background of the "cold war" and internal Arab tensions. Most notable among these latter is the Palestine problem. What happened in June 1967 cannot be understood without understanding the Palestine problem.

It is important to begin with the fact that the problem in the Middle East which now concerns the world in dramatic form is really 50 years old. On November 2, 1967, there were a number of events celebrating the 50th anniversary of the Balfour Declaration. The June 1967 war had its origins in that unilateral proclamation by the British government which was issued on November 2, 1917.

The Balfour Declaration is a vague document on its face. It contains promises to three separate groups: to the Zionist organization, to the Arabs of Palestine, and to anti-Zionist Jews in countries other than Palestine. The present Arab-Israel confrontation and the controversy between

144

Zionists and anti-Zionists can both be simply stated as the predictable, tragic consequences of the failure of Great Britain—and, following 1948, of the United States—to insist upon equal, full implementation of the promises made to two of the three parties specified in the Balfour Declaration. To put it another way, for 50 years the Zionist movement unremittingly pressed its own interpretations of that part of the Declaration which viewed with favor the establisment "in Palestine of a national home for the Jewish people." In this pursuit, the Zionist movement has had the largely uncritical support of people in the Western world. This uncritical support enabled the Zionist movement to pressure Western governments into. support of the clause in the Declaration which made the Zionist movement a beneficiary. At the same time, similar pressures have obstructed or diluted intentions—and sometimes efforts—of Western governments to give full implementation to the intent and substance of the other two clauses which were specifically drafted to safeguard the rights of Palestinian Arabs and "the rights and political status" of Jews in countries other than Palestine. For nearly all of these 50 years this imbalance has produced clashes between Zionism and Arab nationalists in Palestine and a contentious difference of opinion and a quarrel over principles between Zionist and anti-Zionist Jews who are citizens of other countries.

Now it must be clear that forces which can produce hostility and controversy of such duration and intensity are, of themselves, something more than the sentimentality which Zionism, on the one hand, is represented to be, and something more than mere stubborn emotionalism and intransigence which Arab resistance (or anti-Zionist rejection of Zionism) is represented, on the other hand, to be. It is my own considered judgment that there can be no solution to the Palestine problem and no peace in Palestine until the people and the policy makers of the United States candidly face up to the genuine character of Zionism and, either in frank support of it or in adequate opposition to it, confront it as the central obstacle to peace.

When I speak of Zionism in this present political context, I am not referring to the Messianic dreams of Zion—

the restoration of the Zion delineated by the Old Testament Prophets—which are respected and are important theological substance to many Jews and many Christians. Both the regulations for this restoration and for governing the restored Zion are—to those who believe in this theology—Divine decrees; and the event itself will take place through Divine power and at a time which is of God's choosing in His judgment of man.

To cite but one of many possible texts to illustrate the *spiritual* character of the redemption which the Prophets proclaimed:

Zion shall be redeemed with justice,
And those that return to her through righteousness
(Isaiah I:27)

The present mundane annexation of Jerusalem may be no better nor worse than other mundane political acts in a mundane political world. It is not my purpose here to make this judgment, but simply to point out that this recent political situation does not represent the redemption which Scripture prescribes.

The Zionism which did come to the Middle East 50 years ago was and is today a movement of modern political nationalism. It has been guided and directed not by clericals nor by God, but by able, brilliant, often unscrupulous political strategists. The idiom of the movement has not—except for camouflage—been that of Isaiah, Jeremiah, or Amos, but that of a 19th century Viennese journalist, Theodor Herzl, of international lawyers, and political and military specialists. What this Zionism is—and has been—is a well-organized movement to persuade the world community of nations by the use of all available instruments of national policy, that all the Jews of the world voluntarily elect to possess a so-called "Jewish nationality." Prior to 1948 and the establishment of the Zionist State of Israel, Zionism argued that this "Jewish nationality" was homeless. Zionism insists that Jews are an unassimilable nationality group which had been and always would be plagued by anti-Semitism.

According to Zionism, the solution of this problem was for the world to recognize in fact and in law a nationality entity called "the Jewish people"; and, in fact and in law,

146

to give this "homeless" nationality entity territorial rights in which it could be sovereign. Once endowed with territory, it would then operate in the interests of this alleged scattered or "exiled" national entity, mobilizing it, Zionizing or nationalizing it and eventually "in-gathering" as many members of the "exiled" nation as possible. In somewhat more political jargon, this Zionism conceives of all Jews as part of a "Jewish people" nationality, possessing nationality rights and nationality obligations to the "Jewish national home," now called the State of Israel. There is Israeli legislation to support this supra-national nationality claim. And there is the Zionist organization, operating in many nations to implement this Israeli legislation.[7]

The point is crucial. The hostility, at least in its origin, was not between Arabs and any Jews who might elect to come to the Middle East as future citizens of a democratic governmental structure for Palestine. The hostility from its beginnings has been between this Zionist political-national answer to anti-Semitism in many nations, on the one hand, and the rising national self-consciousness of the majority Arab population on the other.

The political framework of the conflict was stated with unvarnished candor by Lord Balfour himself in 1919 in a long memorandum to the British Cabinet. I quote the relevant paragraph:

> Whatever be the future of Palestine it is not now an "independent nation," nor is it yet on the way to become one. Whatever deference should be paid to the views of those who live there, the Powers in their selection of a mandatory do not propose, as I understand the matter, to consult them. In short, so far as Palestine is concerned, the Powers have made no statement of fact which is not admittedly wrong, and no declaration of policy which, at least in the letter they have not always intended to violate.[8]

Now the fact is that the Arabs refuse to agree that the rights of self-determination of the majority population so callously dismissed by Balfour and the Allied peace makers in the Middle East nearly 50 years ago are negotiable. And the Zionists claim that in the Balfour Declara-

147

tion, in the subsequent League of Nations Mandate, and the 1947 United Nations recommendation to partition Palestine—and by right of conquest in three wars—the legitimacy of the Zionist state is established and must be accepted. In simple terms, this is the heart of the legal argument.

None of the great powers has ever seriously encouraged an orderly, legal due-process as a way out of the 50-year-old dilemma. So it is not surprising that when those who do control the power of the world evade the moral questions and equities, those with only incidental power take matters into their own hands because they feel themselves victims. Subsequently, during the thirty years or so between the Balfour Declaration and the establishment of Israel in 1948, Palestine was periodically torn by civil strife. Since 1948 there have been three wars, each with expanding threat to the peace of the world. But the crucial point is that neither the civil strife nor the three wars have come close to resolving the fundamental equities which are still in conflict; and there is little evidence that those equities will be confronted now, despite all the ballyhoo about a new era and new power structuring of the Middle East. Furthermore, the great powers are and have been unforgiveably craven and immoral in their approaches while the smaller states who are the direct parties become increasingly victim to forces of desperation and extremism which, to a large extent, they can no longer control.

The irrationality of the situation is apparent in the present *de facto* condition. There are now perhaps a million and a half Arab refugees. Until very recently the Arab states have appeared to be almost incomprehensibly stubborn in refusing to recognize the State of Israel. They said they did not want war and yet sustained a condition just short of war which they claimed gave them the rights of belligerents There is some evidence that this posture has been altered. The facts are still obscure, but on the basis of reliable sources it seems the Arabs are prepared to accept the November 22, 1967 Resolution of the Security Council which, among other things, calls for the "right" of "every state in the area to live in peace within secure and recognized boundaries free from threats or acts of force." This must

148

certainly include Israel. Israel, on the other hand, has still to accept the resolution, which requires withdrawal from territory occupied in the June, 1967 war; and, in addition, Israel insists upon "direct negotiations" or, in other words, de facto recognition before agreeing to any of the other conditions for a peaceful settlement recommended by the resolution.

Israel now occupies territory which it can claim only on the basis of force. It claims it wants recognition of its sovereignty as a state, but it refuses to delineate or it excludes from negotiable items the responsibilities of that sovereignty with respect to obligations for Arab refugees, boundaries, and the status of Jerusalem. It makes full maritime rights through what may well be legally Arab territorial waters into a cause of war. Those rights are challenged by Arabs because either they do not recognize Israel as a sovereign state or they hold that a condition of belligerency exists between the State which is there and themselves. Meanwhile Israel seeks to establish her legitimacy by force and refuses to submit the core of what is called the "Palestine Problem"—refugees, boundaries, Jerusalem—to arbitration or any negotiations except of a direct character. For the Arabs to consent to direct negotiations would be tacitly to acknowledge the sovereignty of Israel *without* first settling the Palestine problem. So the vicious circle goes round and round.

Most important of all, Israel insists that it is "the Sovereign State of the Jewish people"[9] and rejects the idea that it is solely the sovereign state of its own citizens and nationals.

On June 11, 1967, in an interview on the Columbia Broadcasting System's program, "Face the Nation," Moshe Dayan related this orientation to one aspect of the present search for peace, namely the ability of Israel to absorb the Arab population in the recently occupied territories:

Economically we can; but I think that is not in accord with our aims in the future. It would turn Israel into either a bi-national or poly-Arab-Jewish state instead of the Jewish state and we want to have a Jewish state. We can absorb them, but then it won't be the same country.

149

The former Prime Minister, David Ben-Gurion, stated the same proposition somewhat more boldly on another occasion. Since he was not speaking to a chaotic situation created by war, but rather in the context of deliberated long-range policy, he said:

. . . Israel is the country of the Jews and only of the Jews. Every Arab who lives here has the same rights as any minority citizen in any country of the world, but he must admit the fact that he lives in a Jewish country.[10]

This concept of Zionist nationality cannot be overlooked in the historic controversy. For with this commitment Israel cannot—by the admission of its own leaders—deal in political equities with the Arabs. Nor will it satisfy its own national interests, *conceived in these Zionist terms,* with limited boundaries or without the entire city of Jerusalem. For their part, the Arabs have no assurance that any agreement made at a given time with an Israel of a certain date will prove to be viable in terms of the supra-national commitment of the Zionist State.

The basic irreconcilability of a normal, definitively delineated Israel and the abnormal Zionist concept of sovereignty has not gone completely unnoticed by American policy makers. In 1954 Henry A. Byroade, then Assistant Secretary of State, said in a formal policy declaration:

To the Israelis I say that you should come to truly look upon yourselves as a Middle Eastern state and see your own future in that context rather than as a headquarters, or nucleus so to speak, of world-wide groupings of peoples of a particular religious faith who must have special rights within and obligations to the Israeli state. You should drop the attitude of the conqueror and the conviction that force and a policy of retaliatory killings is the only policy that your neighbors will understand. You should make your deeds correspond to your frequent utterance of the desire for peace.

To the Arabs I say you should accept this State of Israel as an accomplished fact. I say further that you are deliberately attempting to maintain a state of affairs delicately suspended between peace and war, while at present desiring neither. This is a most dangerous policy and one which world opinion will increasingly condemn if you continue to resist any move to obtain at least a less dangerous *modus vivendi* with your neighbor.[11]

Unfortunately the declaration is not always father to the deed! In this case, a tidal wave of Zionist pressures was mounted against the Assistant Secretary and while the declaration of policy has never been repudiated or retracted, it is also true that nothing has ever been done to put it into force.

In the long pull, the immobilization of American power by Zionist influences can serve no constructive ends for the U.S., for Israel, or for the whole Middle East. It endangers —if it has not already irreparably damaged—our national interests. It intensifies the polarization of the Middle East in the context of the cold war, for it leaves the Soviet Union to argue the equities of the political-legal situation while we add patch to patch in an effort to avoid confronting them. It diverts the attention of the rising class of intellectuals and people with greater political literacy in the Arab world, from their pressing domestic social and political problems. It corrodes the faith of this leadership group in the credibility of the United States as an influence for morality and law in world politics. And it aggravates the internal Arab conflict between the revolutionaries and conservatives, for to avoid a confrontation of the fundamentals in the Arab-Israel problem the United States uses whatever influence it has in order to extract more and more concessions from the conservatives. Each time we have encouraged a moderate to believe that we will use our influence to persuade Israel to normalize its relationships to the Middle East, our next move seems consistently to be acquiescence in a further demonstration of the Zionist orientation. As a result, we create one more casualty among Arab moderates, leaving a position of leadership to be taken by some more radical person or movement. This syndrome produced Ahmed Shukairy and his Palestine Liberation Army. It is in my opinion doubtful if in all the jungle of world politics, power-struggles, intrigues, and cynicism, there is a more exasperating syndrome. I also doubt if there is one of comparable im-

151

portance which would be easier to move towards resolution by a few acts of simple political courage.

Dr. Richard Nolte, the ill-fated United States Ambassador-Designate to Cairo at the time of the 1967 crisis put it well in a statement published on September 24, 1967 in *The New York Times*. As one of six steps recommended to American policy makers, Nolte said:

> . . . while continuing to allow private citizens to send funds to individual countries, grant them tax exemptions only for 'strictly humanitarian' donations. . . .

The reference could be only to the United Jewish Appeal funds which the 1963 Senate investigation disclosed provided substantial support for Zionist operations in the United States.

Amplifying, Nolte then added:

> Above all, the one-sided official intervention by the U.S. in support of Israel and the overwhelming partisan private support of Americans for Israel have established the U.S. in Arab eyes as the unswerving champion of Zionism, in spite of efforts by American officials to be fair and even-handed.
>
> Under these circumstances, the U.S. policy interventions labor under so severe a handicap that they are mostly ineffective and downright counterproductive.

Somewhere in the future a new Vietnam threatens in the Middle East if the present policies of expediencies are pursued. If we are to match policy with our national interests in the Middle East the American people will need to be more critically alert. The American press has been almost criminally negligent in helping to provide such vigilance. The incumbents and aspirants to elective office have been more culpable. But a vital, free people can re-examine their opinions and conduct. America still has great assets in its relations with the difficult, individualistic, and resourceful people of the Middle East. The proper cultivation of these assets can realize our national objectives which on the whole are held in mutual interest with the people of the area themselves.

152

NOTES

1. *The Forrestal Diaries,* Edited by Walter Millis, The Viking Press, New York, 1951, p. 347. See also pp. 348, 357, 360-361, 363, 371.
2. Lenczowski, George, *The Middle East in World Affairs,* Second Edition, Cornell University Press, Ithaca, N.Y. 1956, p. 350.
3. Hearing before the Committee on Foreign Relations, United States Senate, 88th Congress, First Session, "Activities of Non-Diplomatic Representatives of Foreign Principals in the United States," Government Printing Office, 1963, Part 9 and Part 12, May 23 and August 1, 1963.
4. *Ibid.,* Part 9, pp. 1403-1410.
5. Cordtz, Dan, "But What Do We Do About the Arabs?", *Fortune,* Vol. LXXVI, No. 3, September 1, 1967, p. 75.
6. *Congressional Record,* 86th Congress, Second Session.
7. "The World Zionist Organization/Jewish Agency for Israel (Status) Law," enacted by the Knesset in 1952 and incorporated in substance, in a 1954 "Covenant" signed by the World Zionist Organization and the Israeli Government.
8. Documents on British Foreign Policy, 1919-1939, Edited by E. L. Woodward and Rohan Butler, Her Majesty's Stationery Office, London, 1952, p. 345.
9. Judgment, in the District Court of Jerusalem, Criminal Case No. 40/61, Section 34, paragraph 1.
10. Quoted by I. F. Stone in "For a New Approach to the Israeli-Arab Conflict," *The New York Review of Books,* August 3, 1967, p. 3.
11. Byroade, Henry A., *The Middle East,* The Department of State, Department of State publication, May 1954, p. 11.

153

4.

THE PALESTINIAN
REFUGEES

Professor Albert Hourani, Director of the Middle East Centre at St. Anthony's College in Oxford, England, is the author of several scholarly books on the Middle East and Arab history, among them "Arab Thought in the Liberal Age," "Minorities in the Near East" and "Syria and Lebanon."

PALESTINE AND ISRAEL

Albert Hourani

At the heart of the Middle Eastern problem lies the problem of Palestine: the struggle of Palestinian Arabs and Jewish settlers for possession and mastery of the land. Now that the Powers have been drawn in and a local crisis has become a world-wide one, it is easy to forget the local causes of it; but it is dangerous, for unless they are treated the crisis may return.

The struggle of Arabs and Jews for Palestine cannot be explained by ancient religious hostility. Jews (and Christians) had always lived among the mainly Arab Muslim population of Palestine, and relations between them had usually been correct. But in the 1880s a new type of Jewish immigration began, mainly from Eastern Europe, inspired by the Zionist idea of a Jewish national home; this soon aroused the hostility of Ottoman officials and part of the population.

During its 30 years of rule, 1917-1947, Britain bound itself by the Balfour Declaration and the Mandate to encourage the Jewish national home, subject to the rights of

157

the existing population; immigration increased, particularly after the rise of Hitler, and Arab opposition became almost universal and drew in the surrounding Arab States.

This hostility sprang from the attempt to implant a new society in a land already occupied by an old one. When the settlers came they found a complete society already there: farmers, craftsmen and merchants, ancient towns and villages, religious institutions, a culture expressed in Arabic, a leadership which formed part of the Arab Ottoman elite. The aim of the newcomers was not to be absorbed into it but to create their own society with its farms and cities, institutions, Hebrew culture and political leaders.

In the age of European expansion, other such attempts were made to plant new societies amidst old ones. They always caused strain, but Zionist settlement in Palestine had special features. The new Jewish society, by the nature of the Zionist idea, was to be a complete and exclusive one. Its aim was to create a wholly Jewish economy: land bought by the Jewish National Fund became the inalienable property of the Jewish people and no non-Jew could ever be employed on it.

It is true, the Zionists bought their land. But in the Middle East political power and ownership of land have always gone together, and the Arabs were convinced that if the Jews had power they would seize the greater part of the land. That the Jews *would* take power became first a danger, then a certainty, as the Jewish population grew. Because of the nature of the Zionist idea, the new Jewish society was an expanding society, open to all who wished to come in. In 1922 Jews formed 13 per cent of the population of Palestine; in 1935, 28 per cent; in 1947, 33 per cent.

As numbers grew, the idea of a Jewish national home turned into that of a Jewish State, and this was unacceptable to the Arabs, not only because by the 1930s most of them were moved by the idea of an Arab State of which Palestine would be part, but because in a Jewish State they would have no choice (whatever guarantees the Mandate might contain) except between being a powerless minority and leaving their country.

Some Zionist leaders did indeed talk of a "bi-national State," but attempts at political agreement broke on the question of immigration. The Arabs wanted to preserve the Arab character of Palestine, and so wanted little or no Jewish immigration. The Zionists wanted to keep the doors of Palestine open, no matter what the form of government.

Here lay the dilemma of their policy: they wanted agreement with the Arabs and they wanted unlimited immigration, but they could not have both, and if forced to choose most of them would choose immigration.

The British, who were politically responsible, had no clear or stable policy on this matter. They had obligations to the Arabs and so opposed the idea of a Jewish State; they had obligations to the Zionists and so permitted immigration, not as much as the Jews wanted but enough to make a Jewish State possible. In 1948, unable to reach agreement with the two parties, they withdrew in circumstances which made fighting inevitable, and there happened what the Arabs had feared for so long.

The dynamic, exclusive, alien society which had grown up among them seized power in the greater part of Palestine, with encouragement and help from some Western States, secured control of the land and brought in immigrants on a large scale; and two-thirds of the Arab inhabitants lost their lands and homes.

All wars create refugees, and after the armies have departed the peasants and merchants return to take up their lives again. Civilized Governments accept that they have a responsibility for those who live in the land they rule. But after the armistice agreements of 1949 Israel refused—with limited exceptions—to allow the Arab refugees to return. In a situation like this everything becomes political, and the Israelis made political use of the refugees.

By refusing to consider the refugee problem except in the framework of a peace settlement with the surrounding Arab States, they linked together two matters which had no moral connection; for the return of the refugees was an obligation which they owed not to the surrounding Arab States but to the Palestinian Arabs themselves, as inhabitants

159

of the land they had conquered. To make such a connection was the more tempting because Israel did not really wish the refugees to return. Even at a peace settlement it would only have offered to take back a small number; for what it wanted was to have the land without its inhabitants, so as to settle its own immigrants.

(This policy was made morally acceptable to Israelis and the outside world by the "myth" that the Arabs left willingly under orders from their leaders. No more than the most tenuous evidence was produced for this, and, in fact, the flight of the Arabs presents no mystery. Some left for reasons of prudence, some from panic during the fighting, some were forced to go by the Israeli Army. What had happened this year throws some light on this. It is clear that no Arab Government ordered the Palestinians to leave this year, but a quarter of the inhabitants of the West Bank left in two months—and for the same reasons.)

Nothing could show more clearly that the basic dilemma of Zionist policy was still there. If it wanted land for immigrants, it was sensible to stop the return of the refugees. But if it wanted peace with the Arabs, then it was fatal.

After 1948, the first step to peace was that Israel should recognize its responsibility to the Arabs who lived in its territory but had been displaced by the fighting. Only this could have set in motion a train of events leading towards peace; and only Israel, as victor and beneficiary of the war, could have taken the step. Israel never did so, and its attitude was accepted by the Western Powers. Every year the United Nations passed a resolution calling for the return or compensation of the refugees, but no one tried seriously to carry it out.

The assumption which underlay the attitude of Israel and the Western Powers was that sooner or later the refugees would melt away, absorbed into the surrounding Arab peoples, and then the problem of Palestine would cease to exist. But this was a false assumption. It was not a mass of individuals who fled in 1948, it was the greater part of a society. A common land and language, a common political fate, and the shock of exile created a Palestinian Arab nation. After 1948 it lived scattered.

Allowing for natural increase, by the beginning of this year there must have been rather more than two million Palestinian Arabs: almost 400,000 in the Gaza Strip, 300,000 in Israel, 1,300,000 in Jordan, 150,000 each in Lebanon and Syria. About two-thirds of them were still registered refugees. Many of these had become wholly or partly self-supporting; if more had not, it was not (as was often said) because the host-countries did not wish them to be settled, but because the absorption of refugees depended on the pace of economic development, and this was bound to be slow in the early stages. In no country was their position satisfactory.

In Jordan they had full citizenship, but Palestinians and Transjordanians had not yet been welded into a complete unity, and positions of real power remained in Transjordanian hands; an intelligent policy of development created an economy into which some of them were absorbed, but the refugees formed a third of the whole population, and a country with such limited resources could not absorb so large a number in 20 years.

In Israel, their position was tolerable: they had civil and political rights, but fewer opportunities of higher education and skilled employment than Jews, they lived under strict military control (until a relaxation in recent months), and were virtually shut out of the political community.

Thus the Palestinian Arabs remained in being as a nation which had lost almost everything but was determined to continue to exist: that is to say, to live with one another, and to live in Palestine. After 1948 this was the heart of the "Palestine problem"; the *de facto* existence of Israel was not in serious danger, but what remained to be assured was the existence of the Palestinian nation. Its attitude to Israel was shared by the other Arab nations, for many reasons. The individual losses of the refugees were felt throughout Jordan, Syria and Lebanon, which belonged to the same geographical and historical unit as Palestine, and where almost every family had Palestinian connections.

More widespread still was a sense of human indignity, a feeling that in the eyes of Israel and the West the Arabs were surplus human beings, to be removed and dumped

161

elsewhere to redress a wrong not they but Europe had done to the Jews. It seemed to most Arabs that Western Governments talked in one way about the rights of the Jews and in another about those of the Arabs. They often said that Israel was here to stay; they never said that the Palestinian Arab nation was here to stay. They talked in language of high principles and threats about Israel's right to free navigation; they used a milder language about the right of the refugees to return or compensation. Unwise statements by Arab spokesmen about throwing Israel into the sea were widely quoted and condemned; no one seemed to care that Israel had, in fact, thrown a large number of Arabs into the desert.

Together with this went an almost universal fear. So long as it could maintain Western standards of technology and hope for wide support in Europe and America, there would be a danger of its expanding into the territory of the surrounding States. Sooner or later, most Arabs believed, Israel would absorb the rest of Palestine, and perhaps parts of southern Syria and Lebanon as well; for a second time the Palestinians would have to move out, and would find themselves walking down the road to Jericho or scrambling across the Jordan bridges.

Whatever their differences on other matters, the Arab States were united in their attitude to Israel, and attracted the support—within limits—of most Afro-Asian and communist States. But coalitions are fragile, in particular if they include States of unequal strength. The common object which brings them together becomes entangled with the separate interests and claims of each, and it was this which led the Arabs into statements and acts which were self-defeating. The essential point of their propaganda was justice for the Palestinian Arabs.

Before 1948 it had been possible to argue that a Jewish State should not be set up because this would be unjust to the Arabs; but once Israel had become a member of the UN, to talk in terms of its disappearance as a State was to embarrass allies and touch a sensitive spot in the European conscience. The official policy of the Arab States was not to destroy Israel but to return to the settlement of 1947-48

162

and a fulfillment of all the UN resolutions; but at the same time they insisted they were still in a state of active belligerency.

This was a dangerous policy for a weaker party to adopt towards a stronger: it gave Israel a license to attack whenever it could claim that its interests were in danger. Israel indeed always remained balanced between two policies: it wanted peace with the Arabs if it could obtain it on its own terms; but war with the Arabs might give it better frontiers.

An Arab policy based on inferior power but expressed in extreme terms played into Israel's hands. This was shown clearly in the events of May and June. For 10 years Egypt and Jordan had kept their frontiers with Israel quiet, and there is no reason to think they wanted a change. But the Syrian frontier was disturbed because of the difficult problem of the demilitarised zone.

Syria began supporting Palestinian activist groups; Israel replied, first by an unprovoked attack on Jordan, not Syria, then by threats which constituted a challenge to Egypt. Egypt replied by sending its Army to the frontier. In so doing Egypt acted as prisoner of the hopes it had aroused, but clearly it did not expect to fight. Egypt's acts were directed towards a political settlement, and its mistake was to think not that the Russians would support it more than they did, but that the Americans would restrain Israel more than they did—that the United States could or would force Israel to give Egypt a victory which might lead to further demands.

Israel called the Egyptian bluff in circumstances which brought it the greatest possible support in the Western world, not only because of Egypt's bad relations with the U.S. and Britain but because of foolish statements by Arab leaders skillfully used by Zionist propaganda.

The frightening wave of anti-Arab feeling which swept Europe and America in June is not the subject of this article. Ordinary people, Jews and non-Jews, certainly felt that Israel was threatened with destruction. It is more difficult to believe that the Israel Government thought so, knowing its own military strength and that it had a guarantee (implicit or formal) from the strongest Power in the world. However that may be, the defensive war soon became a "defensive-offensive" one, and once more what the Palestinians had feared came true.

The Israeli victory has changed many things in the Middle East, but it has not changed the problem of Palestine. The Palestinian Arab people are still there, still in ruin and exile, still determined to exist. Perhaps two-thirds of them are now under Israeli rule; many more refugees have been created, and it is not certain that Israel will allow most of them to return; many who are not refugees have been ruined by the occupation of half of Jordan; every individual Palestinian has now suffered or lost something because of Israel.

The attitude of the Palestinians towards Jordan may well have changed, and if the West Bank is returned Jordan may become a more solid and united State. But in spite of Israeli hopes and efforts, there is no reason to believe that the attitude of Palestinian Arabs towards Israel has changed, except to be hardened by new losses. The Arab States have more and not less reason to think of Israel as an expansionist State which, with the help or acquiescence of the U.S., may dominate politically and economically the region lying between Nile and Euphrates.

It seems not impossible that the Arab States will be persuaded to make a declaration of non-belligerence and the Israelis to withdraw from the conquered lands. Even so, the basic dilemma of Israeli policy remains. The Palestinian Arabs are the estranged neighbors with whom Israel must be reconciled if it is to become "like all nations"; and it remains true, as it has been since 1948, that the first step towards a stable *modus vivendi* is one which only Israel can take—to accept its responsibility towards the indigenous people of the land it controls, and to grant the refugees the right of return or compensation.

In the long run it may be in Israel's interest to do this: only as a mixed State has it a chance of being accepted by its neighbors. But in the short run, the desire for security and for further immigration works against it. It seems more likely than not that Israel will do nothing. If so, it may stay in Gaza and the West Bank; part of the Arab population may be squeezed out; the rumpt of Jordan may be absorbed into some other State; and in a few more years the Palestinian Arab nation may rise once more to haunt Israel, this time inside as well as outside its frontiers.

Harry N. Howard is Professor of Middle East Studies in the School of International Service, the American University, Washington, D.C. A retired U. S. Foreign Service Officer, he served as Acting Representative on the UNRWA Advisory Commission during 1956-61 and as Special Assistant to the UNRWA Commissioner-General during 1962-63. Author of "The Partition of Turkey," "The Problem of the Turkish Straits" and "The Kin-Crane Commission" and other works, he has recently completed a book on "UNRWA and the Arab Refugees."

This article of the refugee problem is modified and updated from an article in "Mid East," Vol. 7, No. 8 (October, 1967).

THE PROBLEM OF THE ARAB REFUGEES: AS YET NO MODERN SOLOMON

Harry N. Howard

The blitzkrieg of June 5-11, 1967, once more threw Middle East tensions into sharp relief, highlighted the problem of the Arab refugees, brought it again into the focus of international attention and added some 350,000 to the relief burden in that troubled area. For a moment, if only for that flickering instant, it fathered the thought, at Western wishing wells, now that Israel had inherited some 800,000 Arab refugees in Gaza Strip, the Jerusalem area and the West Bank of the Jordan, that the problem, by some financial, technological and organizational magic, might be pushed toward quick and easy solution, largely through large-scale projects for development and resettlement. For those acquainted with this problem the story had a very familiar ring. In the earlier years, immediately after the Arab-Israeli conflict of 1948, it had been thought that, following a peace settlement, the refugee problem would soon go away. During the years 1952-1955, large-scale development projects, and especially the Jordan Valley Project, which was accepted neither by Israel nor by the Arab States, were to bring about a solution, and the Middle East would settle down in an era of peace, orderly progress and prosperity. No modern Solomon, nevertheless, in all his wisdom, has yet come forth to relieve the Middle East of one of its basic problems or the international community of its burden.

Origins of the Problem

The problem of the Arab refugees came into being as a result of the partition of Palestine, recommended in the resolution of the UN General Assembly of November 29, 1947, and the subsequent Arab-Israeli conflict in 1948, when Arabs left, fled or were driven out of their homes in Palestine. While it is true that, in some instances, Arab inhabitants of Jewish-occupied regions in Palestine were "invited" to remain where they were, there were others in which they were terrorized into flight, as in the case of Deir Yasin. There is no probative evidence that the refugees were urged or "ordered" to leave their homes by Arab leaders, whatever the myths and the propaganda to the contrary, and none has been brought forward. The fact of the conflict itself, the consequent insecurity and the uncertainty and confusion as to the future were, no doubt, basic elements in the flight which produced the refugee problem. An estimated 725,000 Palestinian Arabs had become refugees in 1949. These unfortunate people lost their homes, their property, their livelihood and their country. They were a community, and, as UN Secretary-General U Thant has recently reminded us, like "people everywhere," they "have a natural right to be in their homeland and to have a future."[1]

Peace Positions

There has been little indication since 1948 that either Israel or the Arab states were ready for any formal peace settlement of the more general Palestine problem or that of the Arab refugees, since the minimum requirements on either side were greater than the other was willing to concede. Under Resolution 194 (III) of December 11, 1948, the UN General Assembly established a Conciliation Commission for Palestine to assist the parties toward a settlement, but, while it produced a general formula in September 1951, this was not acceptable to either side. During the years which followed, the Conciliation Commission was able only to register some 450,000 claims for Arab abandoned property in Israel, and to unfreeze some $10,000,000 in blocked Arab bank accounts in Israel.[2] While the Commission sent Dr. Joseph E. Johnson, President of the Carnegie Endowment for International Peace, as Special Representative to the Middle East in 1961 and 1962 in an attempt to find adjustments in the refugee problem, there were no positive achievements in this direction.[3]

Prior to the 1967 *blitzkrieg,* Israel demanded recognition of its right to national existence, and rejected any major border changes, any alteration in the status of Jerusalem as the capital of Israel, and any large-scale repatriation of Arab refugees to their former homes. On the other hand, the Arab states and the refugees themselves publicly demanded restoration of the boundaries established under the Resolution of November 29, 1947, and the free choice of refugees either of repatriation or individual compensation for those who did not choose to return, under Resolution 194 (III), reaffirmed annually since 1948, and rejected resettlement and integration within the Arab States.

With Israel now in occupation of the Sinai Peninsula, the Gaza Strip, the Jerusalem area and the West Bank of the Jordan River, and the Golan heights, the position of that government, although not officially and formally defined, has undoubtedly hardened. Israel seems likely not only to maintain an adamant position against repatriation of refugees, but to hold on to occupied territory despite the resolution of the Security Council on June 14 and of the General Assembly on November 22, 1967. The Arab states have demanded withdrawal of Israeli forces from newly occupied areas, while also maintaining their previous position, although *de facto* adjustments are possible.

Status of Refugees

While there has been a continuing deadlock on the political plane, under the surface, much "solid, constructive progress" was made since 1948 in dealing with the social and economic aspects of the refugee problem, as both UN Secretary-General U Thant and UNRWA Commissioner-General have recently pointed out.[4]

The widespread assumption that the refugees have been

169

stagnating in idleness in the refugee camps throughout all these years is untrue. Nor is there validity in the widespread belief that, because many of the refugees (in fact less than 40 per cent of the total) were still living in camps so many years after their displacement from their homes, therefore no progress had been made towards their rehabilitation. These mistaken assumptions have given rise to the equally mistaken view that UNRWA was engaged in an endless operation of merely keeping the refugees alive to remain a charge on the charity of the international community. Finally, there is a widespread belief that the host Governments have been deliberately and inhumanely keeping the refugees in a state of destitution and dependence on international charity as a weapon in the prosecution of their political aims. This also needs correction. Although the host Governments have opposed mass schemes of direct re-settlement, on the grounds that this would be contrary to the interests and expressed wishes of the refugees themselves, their record in promoting the rehabilitation of the refugees as individuals through education, training and employment has been notably humane and helpful. They have extended this aid to the refugees in spite of the grave difficulties which already confronted them in providing a livelihood for their own rapidly expanding populations.

The truth is that, up to the time of the recent hostilities, a slow but steady process of rehabilitation had been at work among the refugees and, in recent years, had begun to make an evident impact in improving their economic and social condition. . . . The process of re-habilitation was being achieved not by ambitious and costly works projects and schemes of mass resettlement but by the operation of normal economic and human factors. . . .

By the fall of 1967, there were 1,351,235 Arab refugees on the UNRWA registration rolls, of whom 863,470 were full ration recipients, as compared with 957,000 when UNRWA assumed its responsibilities on May 1, 1950. Geographically, these were distributed as follows:[5]

	Full Rations	Total Registration
Jordan		
East Bank	169,292	288,192
Israel-occupied Territories		
West Bank	193,915	327,933
Jerusalem	61,882	106,658
Gaza	233,864	319,755
Lebanon	104,984	162,330
Syria	99,533	145,647
Grand Totals	863,470	1,351,235

About two-thirds of the refugees are in the age group of 1-25 years, 24 per cent in that of 25-50, and 12 per cent 50 years or above. Some 35,000 reach maturity annually. About 66 per cent of the refugees, prior to June 1967, were eligible for UNRWA rations and services, 26 per cent were eligible for services, and it was estimated that about 8 per cent were self-supporting. About 40 per cent of the refugees lived in UNRWA centers, although the average varied, and in Syria, for example, less than 16 per cent do, as compared with about 65 per cent in the Gaza Strip, 44 per cent in Lebanon and 32 per cent in Jordan.

Granted the underdeveloped state of their economies, it is altogether a problem, despite the myths propagated to the contrary, that the Arab host countries absorbed as many employable refugees, most of whom were farmers, as was possible during the period since 1948. From the standpoint of sheer numbers, Jordan, where the refugees are citizens and made up about one-third of the population, constituted the basic problem, primarily because of Jordan's economic inability to integrate them. While the population density of Jordan as a whole was only some 41 per square mile, that in the Jordan Valley, which represented the basic agricultural economy of the country, was more than 1,000. The problem in Lebanon is one of the most difficult, especially in view of the confessional character of the state, with Muslims and Christians in indelicate balance, since approximately 95 per cent of the refugees are Muslim. In addition, Lebanon has a commercial economy. In Syria, economic integration of the refugees into the economy has moved forward, with substantial assistance from the Syrian Government, although the political issue has remained. In the Gaza Strip, with refugees constituting about 70 per cent of the total population of more than 400,000 and a density of some 3,600 per square mile, the problem defied solution outside a general political settlement.

UNRWA: Not to "Solve" the Problem

UNRWA, or the United Nations Relief and Works Agency for Palestine Refugees in the Near East, the international agency responsible for the welfare of the Arab refugees, came into being on May 1, 1950, on the basis of a resolution of the UN General Assembly of December 8, 1949. Prior to that time, the needs of the refugees had been met through the Disaster Relief Project and voluntary agencies like the International Committee of the Red Cross, the League of Red Cross and Red Crescent Societies, and the American Friends Service Committee, whose activities were coordinated by the United Nations Relief for Palestine Refugees (UNRPR, 1949-1950). UNRWA was not established to "solve" the refugee problem, much less the more general Palestine question. As defined by the resolutions of the UN General Assembly, its functions were and are to provide relief, medical care and education for refugees, and to assist them to become self-supporting. These services have been rendered efficiently at an average cost of some $37 per capita per year, or about 10 cents per capita per day!

UNRWA is today the largest of the United Nations subsidiary agencies, with a staff of some 11,600, 98 per cent of whom are themselves Palestinian refugees. There are some 100 international staff members. About 5,000 are engaged in education and training, and some 3,200 in the health service. The Commissioner-General is an American, Dr. Laurence Michelmore, and the Deputy Commissioner-General, Mr. John Reddaway, is British.

The annual UNRWA budget has averaged some $37,000,000 in recent years, with 45 per cent going to relief services, 13 per cent to health, and 42 per cent to education and training. Thanks to the failure of contributions to match expenditures, by 1966-1967 there was a threatened deficit of more than $3,500,000 even before the June *blitzkrieg* had added the increased burden of some 350,000 refugees who needed emergency international assistance.

Leaving aside the new emergency and its possible consequences, there can be no doubt that UNRWA has contributed much to such stability as existed in the Middle East, as did UNTSO and UNEF, which operated in the security field, and helped to maintain a climate in which social, economic and political forces which might meet the problem in its various aspects might work effectively. While UNRWA deals with some of the most intimate and complicated problems falling ordinarily within the essentially domestic jurisdiction and concern of the host governments, cooperation generally has been very good, despite very natural misunderstandings between the host governments and UNRWA relative to the latter's routine operations.

Because a major portion of its work has been devoted to relief, with all the connotations involved in the term, the technical assistance aspects of UNRWA's work often passed unnoticed, especially in the fields of public health and education and training.[6] In 1950 there was a prospect that UNRWA might develop into a major United Nations center for Middle Eastern technical assistance. While events did not, in fact, develop in that direction, some aspects of the UNRWA programs in education and training have become models to which the wise and prudent in the area might well repair. It is not generally realized, for example, that by 1967, there were some 147,500 children in 440 UNRWA schools in the various host countries, and a total of some 246,500 refugee children were assisted by UNRWA in elementary, preparatory and secondary education. Nor is it known that, by 1967, UNRWA had assisted some 825 students, at an average cost of $500 per student per year, through Middle Eastern universities, many at the American University of Beirut, of whom 160 were graduated in medicine, and 150 in engineering, to say nothing of other skills, *i.e.,* in skills and knowledge desperately needed in the Middle East. Somewhat better known were the ten technical, vocational and teacher training centers, which by 1967 had a capacity of some 3,600 students, and an annual output of some 2,000, with training as teachers and as workers in the building, electrical, metal and automotive fields as well as in business and office practice. By 1967 some 10,000 refugee young men and women had received these various types of training, most of whom had found suitable employment. This was technical assistance of a very high order, even if it did not, and could not, solve the larger refugee problem.

Contributions to UNRWA

During the period since 1948 some $600,541,487 have been contributed to the relief and rehabilitation of the refugees, primarily through UNRWA, whose total income by the end of 1967 was $600,513,407. The United States had contributed some $427,218,069 by the end of 1967, the United Kingdom more than $100,000,000, Canada $22,000,000 and France about $15,000,000. The Arab Governments themselves contributed some $12,000,000 to the UNRPR and UNRWA during this period and, in addition, with their direct assistance to the refugees, contributed in the neighborhood of $90,000,000 to $100,000,000 in cash, goods and services. The government of Israel contributed the equivalent of $256,547 during 1950-1957, while UNRWA had a claim of $375,745 against Israel, largely for losses suffered during the Israeli occupation of the Gaza Strip during November 1956-March 1957. After the *blitzkrieg* and the assumption of new responsibilities relative to the refugees, Israel pledged some $300,000 to UNRWA. Voluntary agencies have contributed some $30,000,000 in assistance to the refugees over the years.

The 1967 Emergency

Following the renewed conflict in June 1967, as noted above, UNRWA was faced with a new emergency involving some 350,000 to 400,000 people who had been displaced as a result of the hostilities, and they found refuge in East Jordan (200,000), Syria (116,000), and the United Arab Republic (38,000). About 130,000 were already refugees from the 1948 conflict. It may be observed, however, that the number in East Jordan is still increasing as more refugees are "encouraged" to move from the West Bank of the Jordan and the Gaza Strip (these being estimated at some 200 per day) to the East Bank. While the Israeli Government indicated in August 1967 that refugees would be allowed to return, only some 14,000 were permitted to do so by the end of August, and only a few have been allowed to return after that date. On February 27, 1968, the UN Human Rights Commission reaffirmed the right of those who had been displaced by the June 1967 hostilities to return and called upon Israel to facilitate their return. The Israel Government ignored this resolution. Following Israeli shelling on the East Bank of the Jordan River on February 15, some 57,000 new refugees were evacuated, and immediately after the Israeli attack of March 21—which was unanimously condemned by the Security Council on March 24— the population was effectively reduced to zero. Most of these people fled to the region around Jerash and Amman. By April 20, the number of refugees and displaced persons east of the Jordan River was estimated at some 605,000, as compared with 332,000 refugees as of June 1, 1968.

But the problem of the Arab refugees is not merely a body of data, statistical or otherwise. As Dr. Michelmore, the UNRWA Commissioner-General, reported in the fall of 1967:[7]

No factual and necessarily brief account can, however, portray the overwhelming sense of bewilderment and shock felt by the inhabitants of the areas affected by the hostilities as the cataclysm swept over them. The disruption of the lives and careers of countless persons, the anxiety caused by the sudden loss of earnings and remittances from abroad, the personal tragedies resulting from the separation of husbands and wives, parents and children, are only some of the problems which confront so many of the former Arab inhabitants of Palestine. They will need the sympathy and understanding of the international community, quite as much as the financial help which has been forthcoming on such a generous scale, as they face the often bitter problems of readjustment which now confront them.

Now UNRWA, once more, was faced with undertaking emergency relief operations on a very large scale, with food, medical supplies, clothing and tents desperately needed, in addition to cash, which provided flexibility in meeting the need. While emergency assistance came from all over the

175

world, largely channeled through UNRWA, the new emergency added gravely to the crippling financial burden which UNRWA was already carrying, and the need for funds to maintain its services was greater than ever.

The problem had not vanished. The Arab refugees had not just gone, conveniently, away. There were now more refugees than ever, and urgent emergency needs had to be met, and there were those who helped to meet it.[8] On June 14, the UN Security Council unanimously called upon the government of Israel "to ensure the safety, welfare and security of the inhabitants of the areas where military operations" had taken place "and to facilitate the return of those inhabitants" who had "fled the areas since the outbreak of hostilities." At the same time, Israel signed an agreement with UNRWA to facilitate its humanitarian work in the occupied areas. There was evidence, however, that this resolution was not being implemented in good faith.[9]

There was much discussion of the plight of the refugees in both the Security Council and the General Assembly, especially in the fall of 1967, when the latter body considered the work of UNRWA. Moreover, in his address of June 19, when he laid down the basic policy of the United States relative to the Middle East, President Johnson called for "justice for the refugees," and added:[10]

A new conflict has brought new homelessness. The nations of the Middle East must at last address themselves to the plight of those who have been displaced by wars. In the past, both sides have resisted the best efforts of outside mediators to restore the victims of the conflict to their homes or to find other proper places to live and work. There will be no peace for any party in the Middle East unless this problem is attacked with new energy by all and, certainly, primarily by those who are immediately concerned.

While this was an over-simplification of a very complex problem, in the origins of which the United States played a very significant role, it did highlight its importance. No doubt plans and projects for a "solution" of the problem would be forthcoming.[11] Meanwhile, however, the problem has remained and grown in proportions and there was little

176

prospect of immediate adjustment. Granted the tragedy, the world was fortunate in having an international agency like UNRWA ready and competent to deal with the refugee problem. If UNRWA could not "solve" the problem, it could meet very real needs, well and efficiently, as it had met similar needs and emergencies since 1948.

NOTES

[1] Introduction to the Annual Report of the Secretary-General on the Work of the Organization, June 16, 1966 to June 15, 1967, U.N. Doc. A/6701/Add. 1, para. 49.

[2] See United Nations Conciliation Commission for Palestine Reports, U.N. Docs. A/AC.25/W.82, Revs. 1 and 2 (1961) and W/84 (1964). The Israelis owned only 6.7 per cent (approximately 460,000 acres) of the land on which they lived at the time of partition in 1947. Arab refugee property in Israel has been unofficially evaluated at some $1,500,000,000. No compensation has been paid.

[3] Joseph E. Johnson, "Arab vs. Israeli: A Persistent Challenge," *Middle East Journal,* Vol. 18, No. 1 (Winter 1964), 1-13; *Issues,* Vol. 18, No. 4 (Summer 1964), 1-13.

[4] See especially U.N. Docs. A/6713, paras. 53-54; A/6787, paras. 32-34.

[5] UNRWA, Registration Statistical Bulletin for the Third Quarter 1967, No. 3/67, Table 1, illustrating situation as of September 30, 1967. All told UNRWA operated 54 centers by June 1967, with 25 in Jordan (most of which are now in Israeli-occupied territory), 8 in the Gaza Strip (Israeli-occupied territory), 15 in Lebanon, and 6 in Syria. Ten tented camps had to be established in Jordan as a result of the *blitzkrieg.*

[6] See U.N. Docs. A/7060; E/CN. 4/L. 1008, 1040.

[7] U.N. Doc. A/6713, para. 24.

[8] See, for example, *Report of a Middle East Trip (July 23-28, 1967),* by L. Emmett Holt, Jr., M.D., President, American Middle East Rehabilitation, Inc. (AMER); *Friends in NEED* (Beirut, UNRWA, 1968), 19 pp.

[9] See, for example, U.N. Doc. A/2713, paras. 24-66; A/6701/Add. 1, A/6787, A/6793, A/6797.

[10] For text see Department of State Publication 8629, *United States Policy in the Near East Crisis* (Washington, D.C., USGPO, 1967), 16-17. See also the documentation in *The Department of State Bulletin,* Vol. 57, No. 1486 (December 18, 1967), 834-844, and the address of Under Secretary Eugene V. Rostow, December 8, 1967, in *ibid.,* Vol. 58, No. 1489 (January 8, 1968), 41-48.

[11] The well-publicized Israeli "plan" did not materialize when Ambassador Comay addressed the Special Political Committee of the General Assembly of the United Nations on December 14, 1967 (see U.N. Doc. A/SPC/SR. 588, pp. 2-8 and verbatim text).

5.

CLERICAL OPINION ON THE CONFLICT

Dr. Willard G. Oxtoby, Professor in Yale University's Department of Religious Studies, is a Presbyterian minister and a specialist in the religious history of the Middle East.

180

CHRISTIANS AND THE MIDEAST CRISIS

Willard G. Oxtoby

When is attack not aggression? When it is self-defense. And self-defense, it seems, has all along been the position of both Moshe Dayan and Gamal Abdel Nasser, of Israeli and Arab alike. Though the shooting has stopped (at least for the time being), the war of words goes on in the continuing story of the Middle East as it has done for decades. From the United Nations and diplomatic circles, from pulpits and editorial pages issue appeals to the principles of morality, decency and justice. Speaking individually or officially, people agree that self-defense is legitimate but differ as to whether particular acts in the recent Arab-Israeli war were self-defense. They agree that there has been more than enough violence but disagree as to the steps to be taken to forestall further violence.

In the Arab-Israeli clash of 1967, the combatants were primarily Jew and Muslim, and political leaders on both sides appealed to religious sympathy and tradition and skillfully manipulated these in support of the war effort. But this was Christendom's war too; or at least a fair number of people were trying to make it so—morally if not theologically.

Christian leaders have been called on, and no doubt will continue to be called on, to adjudicate the moral issues of the Holy Land. They form a "third party" in the bargaining, though they are far from being as disinterested as one might wish. A typical pro-Israeli appeal to Christians was the three-quarter-page ad published in the *New York Times* on Sunday June 4, the day before the Israeli attack. Headed "The Moral Responsibility in the Middle East"— the moral responsibility being "to support Israel's right of passage through the Straits of Tiran"—the ad declared that the threat to peace lay in "the recent Arab military mobilization along Israel's borders." "Let us recall," the ad continued, "that Israel is a new nation whose people are still recovering from the horror and decimation of the European holocaust." As the next six days were to prove, Israel was not so decimated that it had not been able to mobilize an army of men—and women! Presumably the signers of the ad—including such luminaries as John C. Bennett, Martin Luther King, Reinhold Niebuhr and Robert McAfee Brown— did not view Israel's own mobilization as a threat to peace.

That Israel took the offensive in the war only increased the pressure on Christian leaders for moral support. In city after city, representatives of the churches were called on to share the platform at meetings and rallies with rabbis and public officials and to affirm that Israel's cause was just. Clergymen were urged to assert what only a jurist or a Near Eastern specialist could competently assert, that the Israeli attack was not aggression but legitimate self-defense.

This is nothing new. Over the years pro-Israeli interests have systematically cultivated the Christian clergy. Until the mid-'50s, when it was exposed as a Zionist front and so discredited, the so-called American Christian Palestine Committee worked unremittingly to convince church leaders of Israel's moral and biblical claims to the territory she won by force of arms in 1948. Clergymen were offered free trips to the Holy Land, and during the past decade other agencies have continued an Intourist-type treatment for ecclesiastical

V.I.P.s visiting Israel. Thus we have a generation of church leaders schooled not to raise questions when Israel's 1948 war is called the "war of liberation." Apparently they are unaware that some crucial and embarrassing facts about that war have been swept under the red carpet.

The Refugee Problem

Of course, there have been appeals from the other side. But these are mainly humanitarian—appeals for the relief, however minimal, of the thousands of refugees and other Palestinian Arabs who lost their livelihood in the war of 1948. (In the past month, incidentally, the number of refugees has increased by perhaps 100,000.) The focus is on the human need for two reasons: first, because it is immediate; second, because it is nonpolitical. Whereas Zionist political and philanthropic activities in the United States go hand in hand, American charitable and educational organizations working in Arab countries feel the need to remain scrupulously aloof from politics, lest there be a legal challenge to their philanthropic endeavors. The net effect is that the churches have been frightened away from any pro-Arab position. The refugees are dealt with as a virtually unexplained fact, and it is left to the individual to ask why they are refugees at all.

Indeed, the churches have been remiss in regard to the refugee problem. When the first phase of the recent war erupted, the church agencies and boards apparently were concerned chiefly for the safety of their personnel stationed in the Arab countries. The evacuation of these people made it impractical for the churches to commit themselves to extensive relief operations. Only on the 13th day of the crisis did timid TV coverage of Christian interests appear. Informed individuals in the churches campaigned here and there, but as of the last week of June official church support for the Arabs in their time of suffering remained seemingly sporadic.

The first public appeal for refugee relief appeared in the *New York Times* on the 20th day after the war began. Paid by private persons, this appeal called for contributions to three secular organizations working through United Nations channels. UNRWA, with an international staff already on the scene, was during the early weeks of the crisis better prepared than the American churches to offer aid; yet it took three weeks to muster support even for UNRWA. Meanwhile, appeals for support of Israel had been broadcast throughout the U. S.

Vietnam Doves as Israel Hawks

The Middle East crisis poses several problems for Christian ethics. One is how to support the desire of both Israelis and Palestinian Arabs for an assurance of national and personal peace and security. Even more difficult is the problem raised by U. S. national interest in the Middle East. Coming after a couple of winters of theological discontent with our military involvement in Vietnam, the question of what should be the nature of our involvement in the Middle East will doubtless prompt lively discussion when seminaries resume classes in the fall.

Comparisons of U. S. policy in the Middle East and in Vietnam have swirled on editorial pages across the land. Seldom have newspapers had so much free copy from professionals. Historian Barbara Tuchman fired one of the first salvos in a letter appearing in the *New York Times* (and also in the *Washington Post*) on May 30. Claiming that Israel, as representing the source of the Judeo-Christian tradition, concerns America more nearly than South Vietnam Mrs. Tuchman argued that our government's standing by while the Gulf of Aqaba was blockaded was "the ultimate paralysis of power." "Futile fiddling" in the "cynical farce" of the United Nations is useless, she said, for "the family of nations is an illusion with which we comfort ourselves like a teething-ring." The fate of the Western democracies hangs on "independent action in support of our stated policy (which) is not intervention, nor is it something to be afraid of."

Three days later the *New York Times* published a reply by David Lelyveld, who described Mrs. Tuchman's "discussion of the issue as a question of American 'prestige' and a battle between higher civilization and lesser breeds" as:

a return to the rhetoric of the era of high imperialism which she usually writes about. What is saddening is that respected public leaders like Martin Luther King who have courageously opposed American actions in Vietnam should now associate themselves with vague calls for American intervention on behalf of Israel.

Now the fat was in the fire. How could the Vietnam dove be the Israel hawk? Most liberal intellectuals, following Mrs. Tuchman, argued that our interests were more seriously threatened in the Middle East. It is astonishing that for three weeks practically no one engaged in the hawk-dove discussion suggested that our commitment to Israel had been, or ought to be, anything less than unlimited.

The issue was put clearly on June 25 by Yale's David Little in his important letter to the *Times:*

> Neither is our commitment to South Vietnam as "minimal" as is alleged, nor is our commitment to Israel as "maximal" as is implied. . . . Our commitments do not obligate us to support, or even to condone, Israel's patent acts of expansionism, particularly against Jordan. . . . Self-defense in both the case of Vietnam and of Israel seems to be a just cause. In neither case may arbitrary expansionism be so designated. . . . Premier Eshkol's recent declaration which implied that Israel alone is "entitled to determine what are (its) true and vital interests and how they shall be secured" . . . is a cynical doctrine that undermines the notions of justice and law.

Why, during June, did so many of our liberals urge American support of Israel? Mainly because they saw Israel as the bastion of democracy in the Middle East. Israel, they declared, is our only friend, a bulwark against Russian influence in the Middle East—despite the evidence that the spread of Russian influence there is a result of America's long-standing favoritism toward Israel. Or, they said, Israel is a showplace of progressive Western ways—despite the fact that the capital required for technology has been uniquely available to Israel and that comparison of living standards in, say, Gaza Strip or Jordan (which have had so much less

U.S. aid per capita) with those in Israel is acutely offensive to Arabs, who would develop a technology if they had the capital. Or again, they said that Israel is the only nation seeking peace in the Middle East—despite Israel's defiance of U.N. peace-keeping efforts for these 19 years, despite the speed with which she seems to have exhausted all alternatives to armed attack when Nasser closed the Straits of Tiran, and despite her delay in matching the Jordanian cease-fire until she had achieved her military objectives.

While Israel was winning the war, Secretary Dean Rusk stated America's position: "neutrality in thought, word, and deed." One wonders whether Washington would have been so calm if the Egyptians had deliberately torpedoed an American ship, if the Syrians had struck deep into Israel, if the Jordanians had systematically demolished an Israeli hospital or looted a museum or executed children at a boys' school. Our "neutrality" was partiality, the effects of which on future American-Arab relations can only be catastrophic.

Christian-Jewish Relationships

Language of this sort, indeed even the mildest criticism of Israel, raises still a third cluster of problems for Christians: Christian-Jewish relationships on the American scene. The current crisis has revealed Jewish loyalties whose passionate intensity few Christians had been aware of.

Note first the genuinely gratifying advances that have been made in interfaith relationships among us. In the past two decades especially, we have witnissed a "coming of age" of the American Jewish community. The old barriers of prejudice have been falling away in most neighborhoods and professions. No longer are Jews "strange" people. Ours has become a religiously and culturally pluralistic world in which Jews are intelligent, talented neighbors. In this we rejoice.

But many of us Christians assume that Jews are almost exactly like us religiously, too—a naive and even pernicious assumption which, though it may seem to make for brotherhood, is based largely on ignorance. What separates Jews and Christians, alike heirs of Moses and the Prophets? Apart from the status of Jesus, not much, we have thought. The messiahship of Jesus is central to the Christian understanding of man and of God. Hence, Judaism appears to be a rejection of the heart of Christianity, a kind of hereditary Unitarianism. But such a view fails utterly to convey a *Jewish* understanding of man and God. To discover the heart of Judaism we must shift the focus from the messiahship of Jesus to the peoplehood of Israel.

The Peoplehood of Israel

In the rich complex of religious connotations attached to the idea of Jewish peoplehood two main themes are survival and suffering. Over the millenniums the scattered people of the Jews has clung to this religious tradition and this sense of national identity as the fortunes of politics drove it from land to land. In modern times the tradition has been realized in the State of Israel. But to the Jew the triumphs of the people are a sign of divine favor and its tragedies a divine testing. Nobody who watched the Shavuoth observances televised from the Wailing Wall in June could miss the note of tragedy underlying the song of triumph. The trauma inflicted on the Jew in 20th century Europe intensifies his feeling of urgency about a homeland, and as long as this feeling is alive there is slim chance of a reaffirmation of the American Reform rabbis' 1885 Pittsburgh platform: "We are no longer a nation but a spiritual community and therefore expect no return to Palestine."

Thus while in the Christian's view the State of Israel is simply a political fact, for many Jews it is also a profoundly religious fact. That explains why by mid-June fund drives for Israel launched in the United States had brought in more than twice the amount she was reported to have spent on the June 5-10 battle. For example, a synagogue in Connecticut contributed the $10,000 it had salted away for its building fund. A Jewish businessman who led in organizing an Israel rally is reported as saying that he didn't know much about the Bible or about Middle Eastern politics but that for him giving to Israel is a *mitzvah,* a religious obligation.

187

For many American Jews, Zionism functions as a defense against assimilation to modern secular culture. They have no particular interest in traditional theology and ritual observance, but their community can achieve a sense of meaning and relevance by rallying around a tangible campaign. American Jews who feel guilty for having escaped the suffering of their European fellow Jews can atone by sacrificing financially now. Israel is the answer to European Jewry's need for a haven *for* everyday life, but it also meets American Jewry's need for a haven *from* the secular embrace of everyday life. That is to say, what is secular nationalism in Israel is piety in America. American Christians, so accustomed to doctrinal formulations of religion, have generally failed to grasp the nature of Jewish loyalty. And in the eyes of their brethren those American Jews who steadfastly object to political involvement with Israel are victims of an unduly spiritual (i.e., American) concept of religion.

Thus we can understand why American Jews view as a personal affront any criticism of the State of Israel. In the eyes of many such criticism amounts to a blasphemous attack on their religious identity, almost as we would regard an attack on Christ. To assert that Israel has no historic claim to Palestine is to deny the Jew's interpretation of Scripture. To assert that Israel has no moral claim to Arab land is to deny the Jew compensation for Auschwitz and Buchenwald and thus to question divine justice. To assert that Israel had inadequate provocation for launching its preventive attack in June is to cast doubt on the fact of Jewish suffering and thereby on the "sacramental theology" which undergirds the fund drives. To suggest that Israel deserves no support from religious men because it inflicted suffering through acts of premeditated brutality is to question the concept of Jewish peoplehood. And, finally, to liken Israel's militancy to the Germans', the annexation of Old Jerusalem to Hitler's *Anschluss,* is the unpardonable sin.

Denunciations from Jewish Spokesmen

All of which is to say that anything short of total commitment to the rightness of Israel's cause is interpreted as anti-Semitism. As a matter of fact, even the grass-roots anti-Semites of the radical right have been silent of late, probably because our "enemy," the Soviet Union, supports the Arabs. All the same, the Anti Defamation Legue of B'nai B'rith, a body generally distinguished for liberality and intellectual integrity, has seemed downright paranoid in the current crisis. For example: Arthur Spiegel, Connecticut regional director for the A.D.L., commenting on William Buckley's protest against the league's monitoring of broadcasts, declared that Buckley "never lets a fact get in the way of his obsessive hatred of the A.D.L."—a remark irrelevant to the crisis at best and a piece of defamation at worst. Again, Arnold Forster, B'nai B'rith general counsel, dismissed Arab spokesman Mohammad T. Mehdi as "an Iraqi citizen who refuses American naturalization" and declared that "as a guest in this country Mehdi should refrain from criticizing activities of its citizens"—surely neither an invitation to examine the substance of Mehdi's statements nor a suggestion that American Jewish comments on developments in Iraq were off limits.

Jewish spokesmen have directed their scorn not only at political conservatives and "irresponsible Arab propagandists"; they have blasted the mainline churches whose clergy have been brotherhood-minded for years. For example, on June 22 Rabbi Balfour Brickner, director of Reform Judaism's Commission on Interfaith Activities—a normally cordial quarter—denounced the "Christian establishment" as silent "on support for the integrity of the State of Israel." To counter "these failures on behalf of the Christian church," he said, "let us first talk about Israel and its role in the life of the Jew. . . . Understanding the very existence of the Jew precedes any interfaith conversations we might wish to have about Christian-Jewish understanding of conscience, morality or worship."

This, then, is the church's dilemma. For many Jews this war is a holy war. But is it therefore a holy war for Christians? In interfaith matters it is one thing to understand, quite another to agree. Anti-Semitism has to do with the spirit in which criticism is given; it must not be equated with the fact of disagreement.

189

Truth vs. Slanted Information

Christians, clearly, have moral concerns besides the concern for interfaith harmony. The concern for truth and justice, in my opinion, overrides the concern for harmony. Hence outright disagreement with Israel's carefully planned conquest of June 1967 is required of us. Christians must defy pressure on them to sit by silently, muzzled by the fear of being called anti-Semitic.

Besides caring for the hundreds of thousands of blamelessly suffering Palestinian Arabs and working to end their suffering through resettling them somewhere (even in America), the churches must look toward the preservation of free speech in our nation, in fact as well as in law. The right of dissent—staunchly defended by religious and secular intellectuals in respect to other issues—has been effectively suppressed in respect to the current crisis.

The powerful pressures which have made it possible for subtle pro-Israeli evaluations to pass as fact in the news have also caused even the most restrained mediating position to be assessed as Arab propaganda. For a time, virtually the only place in North America where the Arabs could be heard was the U.N. Official Washington, sensitive to the opinions of the voters, appears unable to penetrate the smokescreen of Israeli self-righteousness through which the Arab picture comes and seems ready to sacrifice American interests in the Arab world. Included in such a sacrifice would be Christian educational, medical and evangelistic work built up over the past hundred years.

But the Christian losses will not only be overseas. Here in America, church leaders have unwittingly played into the hands of a militant foreign nationalism. So far as they have been victims of slanted sources of information they may perhaps be pardoned—Bennett on mobilization, Eugene Carson Blake on control of the Old City, any Christian spokesman who confers his blessing on Israel's nationalistic excesses. But so far as they have been victims, so far have they cast doubt on the reliability of the church's official judgments.

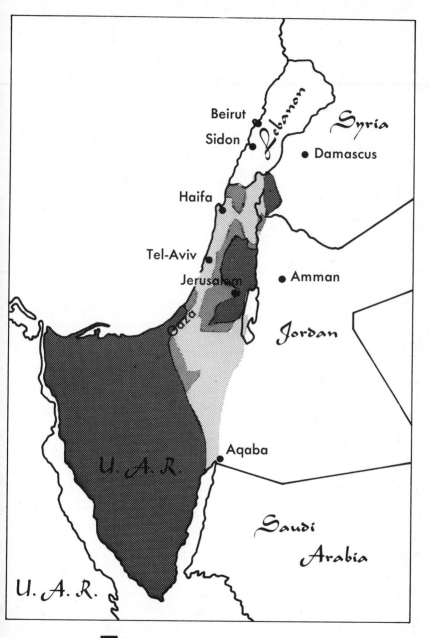

Beirut

Sidon

Lebanon

Syria

Damascus

Haifa

Tel-Aviv

Jerusalem

Amman

Gaza

Jordan

U. A. R.

Aqaba

Saudi

Arabia

U. A. R.

Areas occupied by Israel in 1967.

THE CRISIS IN THE MIDDLE EAST

In the Middle East today the world is paying the price for its willingness to ignore explosive situations of human need and national hatred as though time alone would remove them. The National Council of Churches confesses its participation in this sin of neglect.

In an area which has long seen differing peoples contending for homeland, the state of Israel came into being in 1948. The displacement from their homes of hundreds of thousands of Palestinian Arabs relegated them to refugee status and all too often confined them to misery and despair. For a generation they have cried out for redress of their grievances. Among the few who have heard have been Arab leaders, outraged at the establishment of Israel in the first place and fearful of her future expansion. The churches have also heard. Christians, as well as Jews and Muslims, are closely bound by historic ties to the land where all three faiths had their origin. But our contribution to the relief of suffering and the pursuit of justice there has been inadequate when compared to our resources.

For a generation the world has heard politically inspired threats of a war of extermination against Israel. It has heard answering threats of retaliation by Israel. The consequences speak for themselves. During this period we Christians have said little and done little to seek assurance for Israel that extermination would not be her fate. We have called on neither the Arab states nor Israel to abandon warfare as the means for settlement of conflicting national interests.

Now that violence has erupted, the National Council of Churches will not fail to help those who have suffered. We strive to encourage every means of negotiation and agreement which might remove the causes of violence. This does not mean that we are unaware of the moral claims made by both sides. These claims exist in historical circumstances which are at best ambiguous in a century which has been singularly unkind to Arabs and Jews alike.

The National Council of Churches lists below six major issues which we believe must be dealt with if there is to be peace in the Middle East.

1. *Territorial Integrity*

With due consideration for the right of nations to defend themselves, the National Council of Churches cannot condone by silence territorial expansion by armed force. Israel's unilateral retention of the lands she has occupied since June 5 will only deepen the divisions and antagonisms which separate her from those neighbors in the midst of whom she must dwell.

The territorial frontiers of the states of the Middle East should now be definitely established by negotiation in treaties of peace, and the integrity of such frontiers should be assured by international protection. No territories should be gained or boundaries violated by force. The international community should take all necessary action to prevent territorial changes brought about by other than peaceful means.

2. *The Acceptance of the State of Israel*

Indispensable to peace in the Middle East is acceptance by the entire international community of the state of Israel, ultimately in a peace treaty or by de facto means short of a treaty. Early talks between the belligerents with or without the good offices, conciliation or mediation of a third party are encouraged.

3. *The Refugees*

Means must be found to remove the festering cause of suffering and unrest which is the displacement of the Palestinian Arabs. Israel must accept significant responsibility for solving the refugee problem.

The bringing into being of thousands of new refugees day by day in the wake of the recent hostilities demands

194

the urgent attention of the world. Israel should do everything in her power to encourage such refugees to remain and to facilitate their re-admission to their homes.

We believe possible alternatives for solving the refugee problem of longer standing are repatriation of those who became refugees prior to the 1967 hostilities, to their former homes or nearby, or emigration to other lands of their choice. In either case the refugees should have status of full citizenship and their rights protected. We view these as minimum options to achieve approximate justice, and recognize that these programs will require imagination, patience, and substantial funds. Israel, together with the Arab states and other members of the international community, must share responsibility for solving this refugee problem.

4. *Jerusalem*

We support the establishment of an international presence in the heretofore divided city of Jerusalem which will preserve the peace and integrity of the city, foster the welfare of its inhabitants, and protect its holy shrines with full rights of access to all. We encourage the earliest possible advancement of United Nations proposals to make such arrangements practicable.

We cannot approve Israel's unilateral annexation of the Jordanian portions of Jerusalem. This historic city is sacred not only to Judaism, but also to Christianity and Islam.

5. *Arms Control*

The extension of militarism in the Middle East raises the specter of nuclear confrontation, both between the super powers and, potentially, between the Arab states and Israel. As long as other countries of the world ship arms to the antagonists, either in military aid to establish a balance of deterrence or on purchase orders, the danger of new bloodshed and escalation will remain. We call on all arms-exporting nations to subscribe to the proposal for the establishment of an effective arms-monitoring and control commission in the United Nations. We believe also that arms control is necessary, and that expenditures for armaments should be replaced by expenditures for peaceful purposes.

195

6. *Reconciliation and Reconstruction*

A new will and spirit must obtain, both in the Middle East and in bodies politic around the world, if peace and development are to come to the Middle East. The cruel inequities of wealth, exploitation, poverty, and illiteracy should be corrected, and social changes should be encouraged and supported to that end. Cooperative efforts to utilize scarce fresh water resources such as the Jordan River and practical applications of de-salinization research, are merely two obvious priority needs if arable lands are to be expanded for the benefit of Arab and Israeli alike.

Free trade and with it free access to the Gulf of Aqaba and the Suez Canal by all countries in the area will establish and expand the economies of each nation so that all may prosper. With trade must be coupled capital for investment and construction. We advocate a full-scale development program for the entire area, underwritten by a development bank for the Middle East or by commitments from private or public sources with sufficient capital to join in the endeavor. The establishment of a research institute in Jerusalem or elsewhere, bringing together in dialogue for problem-solving the best minds in the Middle East, Arab and Israeli, would contribute substantially to a plan for growth and a spirit of mutual endeavor. The National Council of Churches stands ready to work with the World Council of Churches, national governments, private foundations, or any interested party for the realization of peace with justice in the Middle East.

We record our conviction that these issues in the Middle East must be resolved in accordance with the principles of the Charter of the United Nations and that the members of the United Nations should fulfill their responsibility both inside and outside the UN in order to bring about such resolution.

Our commitment to the task of peace-keeping motivates us to pursue it across the cultural, confessional, ideological, and national divisions of man. Therefore:

1. We call upon our churches, in the ministry of service and compassion, to support the appeal of the World Council of Churches for an initial sum of two million dollars to be used for relief of all war sufferers through-

196

out the entire area and for resumption of work among the neediest people. Church World Service is to be commended and encouraged to raise one million dollars as our share.

2. Our people should be challenged to support negotiation on the difficult issues. The United Nations peace keeping program must be enlarged to foster international judgment, enabling it to override national sovereignties and conflicting interests to the end that peace may be patiently and finally established.

3. Believing that the present crisis offers further challenge for conversations on international issues with representatives of the Jewish, Christian, and Muslim communities, we encourage the Department of International Affairs to seek and receive every opportunity to involve the widest possible member communion and Council representation for such dialogues.

4. We ask the Division of Christian Unity and the Division of Overseas Ministries of the National Council of Churches to continue to explore with the World Council of Churches the possibilities for an Inter-faith Center in Jerusalem that would be a place for encounter, study and action among Jews, Christians, and Muslims.

5. We commend the World Council of Churches for its program of service and compassion and its mission of fellowship to the area. We offer not only our support but indicate our readiness to respond to their suggestions for ways we can:

a. Testify to the solidarity within the world Christian community.

b. Explore with our Christian brothers in the area appropriate conversation with representatives of the Israeli and Arab communities.

c. Understand the program and needs of the churches and institutions of the other communities of faith.

d. Be a ministry of listening to the concerns of Christians, Muslims, and Jews.

July 7, 1967

> *"Executive Committee of the National Council of Churches."*

197

Licensed in Law and Letters and a graduate of the Political Science Foundation, Mr. Lacouture was Press Attache to General Leclerc and Attache to the Resident General of France and Rabat (1947-49). Former Diplomatic Editor of "Combat" (1950-51) and of "Le Monde" (1951-53) and correspondent for "France-Soir" in Cairo, he has been Head of the Overseas Agency of "Le Monde" since 1957. Mr. Lacouture is also a Lecturer at the Institute of Political Science.

Reprinted from "Ramparts," September, 1967.

MIDEAST PROGNOSIS

Jean Lacouture

Like the Israeli victory, the Arab defeat was too overwhelming to yield beneficial short-term results. On the contrary, everything in the current Middle East situation leads to a pessimistic prognostication for the months, and even the years to come. For the Israelis, one can only predict further military and religious self-glorification, an attempt to exploit their shattering victory to the maximum degree which can only aggravate their contempt for the Arabs. And for the Arabs themselves, the catastrophe scarcely seems to promise any beneficial changes in future policy, since it can easily be interpreted as a stroke of fate, an intervention by mysterious and uncontrollable powers.

The majority of witnesses were struck by Israel's stoicism and unity, by the calmness of the community under the shadow of war and by the sobriety of speeches, as much as by the brilliance of the military action. But many were also struck by the negative aftermath, particularly by the sudden rise in religious fervor. What can be more destructive to a people than to hear it said by their priests that God is on their side, that their victory was a "miracle," that their legitimacy is validated by the sanctity of their cause, their victory justified by their virtue? Political Christianity is dead of "triumphalism"; political Judaism is now threatened.

Militarism, in fact, is Israel's greatest peril because it has been manifested in its most insidious form—the military man in civilian clothing. I. F. Stone, in the July *Ramparts,* theorized that Israel could become the Prussia of the Middle East. This is not really too remote: each civilization breeds its own poison. Those which can cripple Israel are not the poisons of Potsdam, but those of a new cult of power and efficiency. Fantasies of racial superiority need not be clothed in uniform to be diseased. George Marshall was a soldier; Walt Rostow is not. Which one is more militaristic?

To subdue its victory, to avoid the fact that the triumph was that of its "hawks," to think of the objective not as a conquest which should last for the next ten years but as a basis for cooperation for the next 100 years—this is the difficult task confronting Israel. The profile of Moshe Dayan—legionnaire and conqueror—casts a shadow on this pilot democracy of the Near East. As in the United States, militarists prefer to influence power rather than seize it. So the danger is not one of a possible *putsch;* it is rather of seeing Mr. Eshkol conduct himself as the double conqueror of Sinai, Jerusalem, Gaza, and West Jordan.

Nor will defeat be more curative for the Arabs than victory is for the Israelis. The problem of the Arab nations is adapting their actions to their words. Until the recent catastrophe, they lived in a universe of overcompensation, the violence of their speeches tending to veil a deep feeling of division and technical inadequacy. Words, for the Arabs, are not only evasive—they are the trap in which Arabism commited suicide.

What is tragic in this situation is that the Arabs have not yet reached the level of a people who can offset their defeats or humiliations with productivity and economic "miracles" the way that the Germans, the Japanese and even the French have done for the past 20 years. Their only present alternative to inflammatory speeches is devouring meditation. Hence, there is both the beginning of self-criticism in Cairo and a persistance in Arab refusal to see Israel as a reality, a fact of life.

There is a danger that this denial of Israel's validity will continue for some time. Gagged by their humiliation, the Arabs are approaching a time when they will tear each other apart, self-evisceration being their only method of action. This new era will probably witness the crumbling of several of the regimes implicated in the Arab defeat, perhaps even Nasser's, for he is a man whom the masses called back to power but who may not be capable of surviving the responsibility of the disaster much longer. Perhaps a tacit agreement between Moscow and Washington can keep him in power for a while. But the man seems broken, and his enemies both within and without his country are powerful.

The fall of Nasser and/or his allies in the Arab world would not be healthy. It would only aggravate the chaos and create internal conflicts in which terrorism would re-capture the devastating role it played after the first Palestinian war between 1949 and 1952.

The war which just unfolded is deplorable. But it can have two relatively positive consequences. On the one hand, Israel can no longer appear to the Arabs simply as the ghost of Western imperialism. Its own vitality—once hidden behind Britain and France in the disastrous Suez operation—has finally manifested itself. Israel may not seem any less wicked to the Arabs, but it must henceforth be reckoned with as a fact.

On the other hand, Washington's role alongside the Arabs, as well as the limits of French friendship and power, leave no allies for the Arab nations other than the Soviets, however deceptive they may have been. The recognition of Israel, recommended by the West, has only provoked mistrust in the Arabs; but recommended by Moscow, recognition cannot be delayed forever.

It depends largely on Israel whether real coexistence, forced on all parties by the war, will ever produce useful effects. If the state that the leaders of Jerusalem hope to revive in West Jordan is only a protectorate deprived of real dignity, it will merely become a heavier burden to bear during the agitation and terrorism which will surely develop there.

But if the Israeli government allows a truly independent Arab Palestine to be established—including West Jordan, Trans-Jordan and Gaza—then one cannot but hope that a relationship can come about between these two Semitic states, similar to the relations which are possible between India and Pakistan. This is not necessarily an ideal situation. But perhaps it is the road to confederation which certain Arab leaders already privately consider the basis for future negotiations. Before that point is reached, however, one fears that the present hysteria afflicting both sides, Israeli as well as Arab, will lead to violence, death and deception.

An English scholar who lived in Palestine from 1937 to 1954, Denis Baly is now Professor of the Historical Geography of the Middle East, Kenyon College, Gambier, Ohio. He is the author of "Multitude in the Valley," dealing with political problems of the Middle East, "A Geographical Companion to the Bible" and other works.

This article in "The Kenyon Alumni Bulletin" for January-March 1968 issue, was based in part on an article Denis Baly wrote for "New" Magazine (World Horizons, Inc., New York, Vol. 2, No. 4, summer, 1967) entitled "Palestine: Crucible of Conflict."

THE MIDDLE EAST: RECURRENT CRISES

Denis Baly

I do not think that you are going to like what I am going to say, because I have nothing to offer you but "words of mourning and lamentation and woe." Nevertheless, I ask you to listen politely to the end.

I should like to begin with a quotation. It is from the pen of no less a person than Reinhold Neibuhr, and it is dated June 26, 1967. "No better simile fits the war between Israel and the Arabs in lands of biblical memory than the legend of David and Goliath. David, of course, is little Israel, numbering less than 2.5 million souls, which have been forged into a nation since 1948 when the United Nations granted independence to the British Mandate. Significantly, however, Israel won her independence in the 1948 war with the Arabs. Goliath, of course, is the Arab World under Egyptian President Gamal Abdel Nasser's leadership, numbering a population of 20 to 40 million. This Goliath never accepted Israel's existence as a nation or granted it the right of survival. Nasser, who had abolished Farouk's corrupt monarchy after the first Arab defeat, had ambitions to become the architect of Arab super-nationalism. And the

Cairo radio daily blared out threats of Israels extinction."[1]

This is a very popular American view, but it is dangerously wrong. Americans far too easily see the Israelis as deserving immigrants, crowding in past a statue of Liberty, and the Arabs as "Indians," fated for extinction or the reservation. Far too much has been made of the supposed contrast between the hard-working, dynamic, Zionists, and the backward, lazy, Arabs. One has only to glance at the newspaper cartoons to see what the American stereotype of an Arab is: a picturesque, but squalid, figure in a long robe, either astride a camel, or lethargic beneath a solitary palm tree. Admittedly, Arab propaganda is usually pathetic, and often grotesque, but this sorry caricature has neither excuse or validity. Arabs are *not* lazy, as those who have worked with them closely can testify, and if Arab administration is often less than effective, it should be remembered that they are as yet beginners in this long task, having most of them been governed by foreigners for over six hundred years.

It has been instructive, and alarming, to consider the American reaction to the events of June of this year, as expressed in the newspapers and popular journals, and in the spate of paperbacks which one can now see everywhere on the bookstands of the nation. These display a public opinion which is wholly one-sided, blithely unaware that there is any other side to be heard, and quite uninformed by any understanding of tragedy. There is a sense of overwhelming relief, and even something of ecstasy, because the knock-out blow was so swift, because the right side won, because the innocent were vindicated, and because the danger of war was removed. It has been called openly by many people "the Holy War," and the speed of the victory took on the quality of a miracle. The merciful God is thought to have triumphed over his enemies. "Yes, I know that it was unfortunate and it had to happen," many people have said to me, "but how much worse it would have been if the Arabs had won."

I do not share this relief. Ten years ago, after the last Israeli invasion of Sinai, I wrote, "The situation is now beyond hope, utterly and fundamentally irreconcilable, so embittered and so savage has it become."[2] Reviewers took me to task at the time for my pessimism, but what I said then I say again today. I do not abate one whit of it.

My conviction is that, far from the blitzkrieg of last June having solved anything, or resolved any dilemma, there is in the Middle East today a ghastly necessity of conflict, a situation in which both sides feel themselves compelled to violence, each finding no alternative except to renew the struggle, and to renew it on terms more favorable to their own side, that is to say with more powerful and more sophisticated weapons, and more effective destruction. There was a notable, and horrifying, escalation between 1948 and 1956, and again between 1956 and 1967, and the technique of the sinking of the Elath makes clear that escalation is still continuing.

In a conflict of this kind, escalation is inevitable because the people against whom the fighting is conducted are not the real enemy, they are only symbols of the enemy, single instances of a many-headed hydra. Even victory achieves nothing, for the enemy is still there, and the danger as evident as it was before. One has never gained anything more than a breathing space, and is driven next time to use more force in the desperate effort to achieve security. Defeat, of course, all the more obviously forces one to argue that it is necessary somehow to become stronger. In the dread arbitrament of war it is normally expected that the proper application of overwhelming power will bring the struggle to a satisfactory conclusion. For power to be overwhelming it is not, of course, always necessary that there should be total war. Limited force may, possibly, achieve the purpose. But if the purpose is not achieved, greater power is required next time. This power has, roughly speaking, two components: numerical superiority and technical superiority. Where one component is evenly balanced between the two contestants, it is sufficient to be superior in the other.

In the kind of conflict I have in mind, however, neither side has the opportunity of utilizing both the necessary components of victory. In the Middle East at the present time the Arabs lag far behind the Israelis in all the technical resources of war, and this term includes both the hardware, and the highly specialized technical training. Furthermore, they see no hope in the forseeable future of redressing this imbalance. As they see the matter, they are confronted, not merely by Israel, but by the whole western world, by the vast economic and political power of "the Jews," extended throughout the world, and able to tap the limitless resources of the West. The only thing that they can bring to bear is the weight of numbers. They have, most of them, been governed by foreigners for the last six hundred years, and being but beginners in the game, they are lacking in all that is necessary to make these numbers effective—economic resources, technical skills, and political expertise.

But they cannot afford to give up the struggle. The Arabs regard Zionism very much as Americans regard the Communist threat. It is the utterly foreign way of life which has some how gained a foothold in their world. They view the State of Israel very much as the American people would view the establishment by the Communists of a beach-head in Rhode Island or Massachusetts, or as in fact Americans regard the Communist control of Cuba. That both Cuba and Israel are tiny pieces of territory in relation to the enormous expanse which they themselves control is quite irrelevant. It is easy to say that the Arabs should not be so frightened, but few can share another people's fear, and it should be remembered that a large part of the neutral world believes the American panic fear of Communism to be no less foolish. It is also easy to say that the Arabs *ought* to recognize Israel's right to exist, and so, perhaps, they should. But they can see no difference between what they are doing, and the United States' refusal to tolerate the tiny Communist island of Cuba, or to recognize Red China which contains a quarter of the human race. The unhappy truth is that as things stand neither the Arabs nor the Americans can publicly admit the right of the enemy to be where he is, because the admission would seem to them both too terrible and too shameful.

It is very difficult for Westerners to grasp that the Arabs are convinced, and can quote much evidence for their conviction, that Israel is an expansionist nation, whose appetite is still far from sated, a nation which displays all the cunning of the Nazis in proclaiming publicly that she has no more territorial ambitions, while secretly preparing the next aggression. Even at this present time there is much discussion in the Arab World about where Israel intends to attack next. Will it be across the Suez Canal in order to remove Gamal Abdul Nasser finally from their path, or will it be against Lebanon to bring all the headwaters of the Jordan under Israeli control? These discussions may seem fantastic to those who see only the Arabs, and not the Israelis, as aggressive, but Israel has stated publicly to the world that she will, if necessary, fight to get control of the vital waters of the Jordan, and there has been a whole series of highly publicized Israeli (and at an earlier date Zionist) plans to utilize for the irrigation of the Negev not only the Jordan but also the Litani, which is a separate river lying wholly inside Lebanon, notably the Lowdermilk scheme, which received great attention in the early 40's, and the so called TVA plan as late as 1953. Do not be surprised at this. When you live on the edges of the desert water is life, and even inside the United States, when drought threatens, similar sentiments are expressed. On August 13, 1965, when there was a major water crisis in New York and the neighboring states, the New York officials told Secretary of the Interior Udall bluntly, "The 200 million gallons of fresh water we pay out daily into the Delaware River are not water but blood. We cannot be asked to do the undoable."[3]

Those Arabs who remember the Mandate remember also the flaunted maps which displayed not only Palestine but the whole of Transjordan in Zionist blue. They remember how successive Zionist Congresses insisted that "only those actuated by malicious wickedness" could accuse the Jews of wanting a Jewish State. They remember how Sir Laurie Hammond, who had actually been a member of the supposedly impartial British Royal Commission in 1936, which had proposed partition of the country, told a Zionist meeting in London what he envisaged happening to the suggested Arab state. "You will find that the National Home in Palestine, if you can get sufficient in that country to meet immediate requirements as a Sovereign Power, will be the

209

first step, in my opinion, towards getting back into the rest of the country . It will take many years, but it will come."[4] They remember also the official statement of the Twentieth Zionist Congress in 1937, which decided, somewhat tentatively, to accept the principle of partition. "The Debate has not been for or against the indivisibility of the Land of Israel. No Zionist can forgo the smallest portion of the Land of Israel. The Debate concerned which of the two routes would lead quicker to the common goal."[5]

Since the establishment of the State, the Arabs have watched it apprehensively as it acquired territory which had not been allotted to it by the United Nations. They are told that the Knesset, the Israeli parliament building, has engraved upon its walls the biblical promise that the Israelite dominions would extend to the Euphrates. They have seen Israel make Jerusalem their capital in despite of world opinion. The Israeli Yearbook of 1951 spoke of "that part of the country which we so far occupy," and in 1952 asserted that "the State has been established on a small part only of our true homeland." A detailed town plan for the whole of Jerusalem existed in Israel in the 1950's, long before the occupation of the Old City, and rather over two years ago there appeared the official 1:100,000 Survey of Israel, consisting of 26 maps. Two of these, Nos. 9 and 12, contain not one square inch of land inside Israel, but there was nothing on the maps to show that the territory was administered by Jordan, and the heading was still "Survey of Israel."

Moreover, they have seen Israel twice launch its armies across the armistice lines, making no secret of the fact that they fired the first shot, in 1956 with the active support, and prior collusion, of the British and French governments, and in 1967 without this active support from outside, but with modern western weapons, and the terrorizing use of napalm upon an undefended population. They have also, from time to time in the intervals, seen the Israeli army, clearly with government support, make brutal raids upon Gaza, and upon unprotected Jordanian villages, intended to "teach the Arabs a lesson," giving as Ben Gurion said, "two blows for one." It was these attacks upon Jordan which had followed an especially pacific policy towards Israel that convinced the Arabs that none of them was safe, and that they were but a prelude to further violence to come.

It is true that the Arabs conveniently forget how much their own behavior has done to provoke aggression, and how aggressive they themselves appear to Israel and the world outside. Armed marauders have continually crossed the armistice lines into Israel, very often it is true unofficially, but since 1955 both Syria and Egypt have from time to time officially encouraged such raiding in retaliation for the Israeli attacks. Between 1955 and 1956 the encouragement was largely Egyptian, but since then the Egyptian government has been much more cautious, and has indeed been accused by the Syrians of being a "paper tiger," doing very little against Israel, but wasting its energies on fighting Arabs in the Yemen. But of inflammatory radio speeches and of constant incitement to violence there has been no lack. The Arab states have refused even to speak of a settlement, and the Israelis echo the words of the Psalmist, "I labour for peace, but when I speak to them thereof, they make them ready to battle." The bitterness, and indeed the hatred, among the Arabs concerning Israel strikes the visitor like a blow in the face, and it would be merely idle to pretend that this is not so.

The Israelis blame the Egyptians most bitterly for closing the Suez Canal to them, and for seeking to close the Straits of Tiran, believing both to be a clear violation of international agreements about freedom of the seas (though it should be noted that the Egyptians are not without legal support for their view that they have the right to close these passages in their own defense). The Israelis regard Gamal Abdul Nasser as nothing better than a dictator, bent on their destruction, and they have but grim memories of dictators. They maintain that they could reasonably swiftly make peace with Jordan and with Lebanon, if it were not for the relentless browbeating of the Syrian and Egyptian governments, able to squeeze the weaker country of Jordan between them, and bend her to their will. They know, only too well, how many there are in Jordan who are Nasserite sympathisers, and they view with apprehension the

211

open efforts of the Egyptian and Syrian leaders to unseat King Hussein, the most moderate of the Arab rulers. It was exactly this dreaded union of Syria, Egypt, and Jordan, which seemed to the Israelies to have taken place in the spring of this year.

These Arab threats are quite familiar to American readers through the columns of their newspapers, which have given ample coverage to the Israeli case, but one must always remember how much more present and ominous they were to the Israelis themselves, shut inside a tiny country, no more than twelve miles wide at its central waist. The restriction of movement, the closed armistice lines, the potential enemies growling on every boundary, created in the Israeli mind a frustration and a claustrophobia comprehensible only to those who have themselves lived for years in such political straits.

Moreover, just as the Arabs are without any expectation that they can dominate the Israelis by technical ability, so also the Israelis are entirely without hope that they can ever overwhelm their enemy by sheer weight of numbers. Each lacks, and sees no hope at all of ever acquiring, a necessary ingredient of victory, and yet each most desperately fears the victory of the other. Israel has known for years that only by constantly forestalling an attack, and forestalling therefore the advantage which the attacker always has, could they prevent their country being sliced in two; and Egypt is fully conscious that the enemy has only to wait for the completion of the High Dam, and the filling of the vast reservoir behind it, and then to destroy it, to wipe out for generations, if not indeed for ever, the Egyptian nation. As Ian Morison said about the Punjab problem in 1947, "Each (side) suffers from a psychosis of fear, a terror that it is about to be attacked. . . . One of the symptoms of this disease is that each side passionately believes the other to be solely responsible. The outside observer studying this gigantic and terrible phenomenon wonders whether questions of 'responsibility' and 'blame' are not irrelevant. Either all parties concerned are responsible . . . or else there are certain cataclysms in human affairs in which men do not retain control over their destinies."[6]

As with the Punjab twenty years ago, so also here I believe, it becomes irrelevant to ask who is the aggressor and who is the attacked, who is guilty and who is innocent. All are guilty, Arabs and Jews, British, French, Russians, and Americans, and no country comes out of this sorry story innocent, or even with dignity. But it is not irrelevant to ask who has suffered wrong. It is an awful and undeniable fact that unimaginable wrong has been done to Jews by Christians throughout the centuries, and not least in Europe within living memory. And lest it be imagined that this wrong is something of which the people in this country may safely wash their hands, for after all it did not happen here, let us remember the tragedy of how little happened here. Truman's insistence that 100,000 Jewish refugees from Europe be admitted to Palestine in 1948, which received enthusiastic, not to say hysterical, support from the churches of this country, was not matched, either by him or by them, by proposals that a similar number be received here, into a country which was much better equipped to absorb them. One could wish that Christians in the West showed more awareness of this tragic history, which did not begin with the Nazis, but is a story stretching back for almost two millennia of Christian propaganda and Christian beastliness.

Moreover, wrong has been done, not to one people, but to two. Arabs are incensed when public speakers dwell upon the wrongs done to the Jews, but overlook at the same time the wrongs done to the Arabs, not merely the now doubled tragedy of the refugees, but the constant and blatant disregard of Arab opinion, Arab arguments, and Arab unhappiness. Much of the refugee problem must be laid at the Arabs' door, for the unwisdom of their propaganda in 1948 and again in 1967, but very much also in 1948 was it the fault of the ineptness and the folly of the Mandatory Government, and the cruelty and brutality of the Zionists both in 1948 and again in 1967. You may not like this judgment, but you should remember that the stereotypes which we all have about the Middle East are not necessarily accurate. The Jordanian soldier, for example, is not the monster of terror that he is represented to be.

213

He is certainly a wonderful sight on parade, and effective as a fighting man, whom I have found that the Israeli soldiers sincerely respect, but he is by nature gentle, and lacking in that ruthlessness which carries war through to a successful conclusion. The Israeli soldier is a sturdy amateur, fighting with conviction for a cause, and as such becomes in wartime tough, wily, and aggressive, with very much fewer inhibitions about carrying the fight through to an effective end. I think that you should meditate upon this comparison before you repeat too lightly the oft-stated opinion that it would necessarily have been worse if the Arabs had won. It is, I should add, by no means only my own opinion.

You may think that I have been severe upon Israel, but do not think that I am unaware of, or do not sympathize with, the dread compulsion which drives them into the arena. What haunts Israel at the present time, and their leaders are fully conscious of it, is nothing less than the fear that the State will collapse from within, and all the sufferings, struggles, and privations of the last fifty years garner them no more than Dead Sea fruit. I have said that the only thing they have to set against the Arab numerical superiority is the ability to tap much vaster economic resources, and to apply this wealth efficiently because of their magnificent technological achievements. But already 60% of the Jewish population of the country consists of the so-called Oriental Jews, that is to say those who have come from the African and Asian countries. They constitute a serious color problem, and are in fact, though certainly not legally, second-class citizens. This 60% of the population provides only 25% of the secondary school students, since they cannot pay for the education, only 5% of those at the various institutions of higher learning, and only 2% of those who earn an academic degree. It is estimated that in fifteen years' time they will have become 80% of the population and the technological advantage, upon which alone the physical security of Israel depends, and which has been exploited so brilliantly in the past twenty years, will, as far as anyone can see, be no more.

Hence the passionate conviction of Moshe Dayan and his followers, profound believers in the ability of technology to solve all problems, that the technological advantage must be exploited to the utmost now, the frontiers extended to a position of maximum security, all available water resources gathered within the country, and kibbutzim established at every strategic point. There are many in Israel who do not agree with them, and feel their policy will do no more than exacerbate the problem. The expansion of the frontiers for reasons of strategy necessarily means the inclusion of a large number of Arabs, and the increase, therefore, of the number of "orientals," who will, moreover, be hostile to the State. Also, the more the State insists upon secure, because expanded, frontiers, the less secure it will in fact become, since this expansion must of necessity increase the hostility of the Arab States, confirm them in their fears of Israeli aggression, and strengthen their determination to forcibly contend with Israel when the opportunity arises. In the opinion of the moderates in Israel the only hope of peace with the Arabs is to convince them that their fears of the Jews are unjustified, and this cannot be done by the present policy.

Unfortunately, circumstances have conspired to maintain the expansionists in the ascendant, and my own conviction is that Israel does not in fact intend to withdraw from the territory she has gained by force of arms, though the thought of Israel and Egypt facing each other across the Suez Canal fills me with terror.

Other tensions within the State of Israel serve to reinforce the danger of internal collapse. There is the division between the *Vatikim,* the older immigrants who built up the State, and the *Sabras,* the younger generation born in the country, who do not share their tragic experiences, and therefore do not share their purpose or their expectation. There is also the difference between the communal settlements, the *kibbutzim,* and what is sometimes called "the outside," the towns and cities which contain the great majority of the population. The *kibbutzim* symbolize in large measure the original purposes of the founders of Israel, but they represent only a small percentage of the population today. There is a striking difference between the official philosophy, found in the school books, which is strongly

215

collectivist and speaks of the *kibbutz* as the Israeli ideal, and the thinking of the younger generation, which to the *Vatikim* appears dangerously individualist, pleasure-seeking and intent upon the creation of an affluent society. The *Sabras* want Israel to be like the other nations, and this to the *Vatikim* is pernicious assimilationism. The flagging of the pioneer spirit alarms them, and so does the increase of people emigrating from the country, the slowing of the economic development, and all the other signs that the Israel of which they dreamed, and for which they fought and suffered, may in fact perhaps not come to pass. It is an important part of their thinking that Israel is most truly herself when she recognizes that she is always *contra mundum,* "a light to the nations," an everlasting fire which the world seeks constantly to extinguish. The Eichmann trial and the Arab danger have been both exploited in order to impress this truth upon the generation to come. That Eichmann was a conscienceless murderer, and that Arab leaders have spoken again and again of destroying Israel, are undeniable facts, but circumstances within the country have too often led Israeli statesmen to make dangerous use of these facts. "The dirtiest trick the Arabs could play upon us," said a thoughtful Israeli not long ago, "would be to make peace with us."

The danger that the Arab States may realize that they have this card in their hands seems singularly remote, for Arab aggressiveness is flaunted before the world in a propaganda of hate and revenge. Once again it springs from fears and tensions deep within the Arab societies. Gamal Abdul Nasser is far from being the villainous dictator that is his picture in Israel and the West. The Egyptian revolution of 1952 was, and has remained, a very puritan one, bent upon purging the country of corruption and bad government, and no one should decry the extraordinary achievements of the revolutionary government inside Egypt itself. Abdul Nasser is deservedly popular among the Egyptians, and the strange episode of his resignation after the Egyptian defeat, and the universal Egyptian demand for his restoration, was not the play-acting that cynical Western reporters have assumed. His foreign policy, though flamboyant, has been skillful and cautious, and for years he has set his face against all hot-headed talk of actually attacking Israel. The virulent propaganda of Cairo radio was, in fact, a surrogate for physical aggression, intended to reassure the fearful among the Arabs, and frighten away the Israelis. It has been, no less than the Israeli active expansionism, a disastrous policy, for neither the Israelis nor the Arabs are ready to be frightened out of what they believe to be their only chance for survival. Yet in all these years massive propaganda seemed to the Arab governments the only defense they had, the only wall they could build around themselves, even though they knew the wall to be a mere facade. For no Arab state is a Goliath. Instead, all are desperately weak, plagued with economic problems, lacking in skills and resources, tormented by all the difficulties which belong to countries just beginning to govern themselves after centuries of subservience.

One of the legends which bedevil discussion of the Palestine problem is the belief that from the first the Arabs were lusting for battle, and that the Jews were helpless victims, ''a people quiet and unsuspecting.'' Nothing could be further from the truth. *Both* sides, in 1948 as well as later, were fully prepared to fight, in the sense that each was determined to go to war, if necessary, in defense of what were understood to be vital interests, and *both* sides were fully convinced that war might indeed be necessary, to stave off what might otherwise be disaster. The difference has been on every occasion that the Israelis were very much better prepared in materiel, in military training, in careful planning, and in the enlistment of the entire population for the defense of the country. Even in the forties, before the end of the Mandate, there was hardly a Jewish schoolchild who was not an active member of one of the military, or paramilitary, organizations, illegal though these might have been. The Arabs, on the other hand, have only too often been feckless, and the victims of their own propaganda. Their weakness, indeed, has been exactly that they have *not* indulged in the ruthless and thorough preparation of which they have so often been accused, but have believed what they wanted to believe: that when it came to the test their num-

217

bers and their undoubted enthusiasm would win the day.

The error of the Israelis, and this applies, alas, to both moderates and extremists, has been that of all colonialists: they regard the Arabs as backward "natives," capable of understanding no argument but force, and requiring either to be removed, or else to be efficiently governed by some benevolent power for their own good. The error of Egypt has been that of all revolutionaries: to believe that revolution must be exported, and that the breakthrough which they have made must be made in every country. This has led them to inflame the Arab quarrels by their incitements to rebellion, and to saddle themselves with the tragedy of the Yemen adventure.

But Gamal Abdul Nasser, though a revolutionary, is not extremist, and I would regard as one of the greatest dangers at present confronting us, the possibility of his removal. If he is to be allowed none of the "honors of war," if Israel is to remain beside the canal, far inside Egyptian territory and minutes away from Cairo, Nasser may be overthrown, and his place then certainly be taken by a true extremist, dedicated to violence as the only means of salvation.

It is just as much a mistake to lump all Arabs together as it is to regard the Jews as an indistinguishable mass. Jordan, which received in 1948, and has alas received again, by far the greater number of refugees, gave them citizenship, and little by little tried to absorb them into the economy, though the problem was immense, for they were almost half the population. It was a very slow process, but in early 1967 it was possible for those who worked with the refugees to talk openly of resettlement, and to envisage the days when the camps would be no more. Now all hopes are in the dust. Jordan was within sight of becoming economically a viable state, but today she is stripped of all her resources, and laden with burdens too heavy to be borne. When a comparison is made between "the Arabs" and "the Jews," it should be rememberd how much Jordan achieved in so short a time, and with what little prior training, and with what small resources it was done.

The critics of the Arabs argue that Jordan brought the

disaster upon herself, for she was involved in the war by her own decision, and that it was nothing less than folly for King Hussein to make his peace with Nasser. They forgot, I think, the appalling miscalculation of Sunday, November 13, 1966, when Israeli forces, backed by air, tank, and artillery support, launched a three hour attack on the Jordanian Village of Samu', destroying 125 houses, a clinic and a school, and leaving behind them 18 dead and 134 wounded. This had been unprovoked by Jordan, and consequently the Arab world became convinced that the events of ten years before were about to be repeated, and were sure that the Israelis must have once again behind them the backing of one or more of the Western powers, for surely they could not mount an invasion of the Arab world without this support. A wave of panic fear swept over all the border states, and their subsequent actions are explicable only in this light. The hysterical warnings to Western countries not to interfere, and the threats to cut off oil supplies, were intended to prevent, if possible, at the very last hour, that military assistance which they believed to be already promised. After 1956 Western denials carried no weight at all, for their previous denials were now known to be an utter sham, and American and British chatter about perhaps having to intervene to preserve the freedom of the seas suggested that once more a facade of moralism was to serve as the mask for aggression. The fear of Western intervention seems on this occasion to have been unfounded, but, whether valid or nor, it was a fear that gripped the Arab mind. In face of this imminent danger none could stand aloof, and all divisions must be forgotten. Hence the visit of King Hussein to Cairo. Similarly, the Egyptian closure of the Tiran Strait, and the demand that U.N. troops leave her soil, seem, in part, at least, to have been last minute efforts to rectify some of the disadvantages in which Egypt would be placed when the attack took place. It is usually news to Americans that although Israel was clearly the attacker in 1956, the United Nations observers had been placed only on the Egyptian side of the border, Israel having flatly refused to have them on the grounds that it would be a breach of sovereignty. The Egyptians

219

were fully aware, therefore, that Israel was free to make what dispositions of her troops she would, while she did not have this freedom.

It was, of course, a miscalculation no less serious than that of the Israeli attack on Samu', and the six day war has rightly been called a "tragedy of errors." It has now taken place, and the question is, what is to happen next. My own conviction is that this is but the beginning of tribulation, and my expectations for many years to come are sombre beyond all words. Neither unparalleled triumph nor utter desolation can profit a nation. "What can be more destructive to a people," asks Jean Lacouture, "than to hear it said by their priests that God is on their side, that their victory was a 'miracle,' that their legitimacy is validated by the sanctity of their cause, their victory justified by their virtue? . . . Militarism is, in fact, Israel's greatest peril because it has been manifested in its most insidious form—the military man in civilian clothing." [7] Perhaps a *modus vivendi* will be patched up, and certainly there are those on both sides anxious to work for something more enduring. But the bitterness and humiliation of the Arabs is much too profound, and the shock of defeat altogether too recent, to permit most of them at the moment to dream of anything but revenge. They see the recent *blitzkrieg* as a kind of Pearl Harbor, which must someday be reversed, however long this takes.

"My people," said Isaiah, "have gone into capitivity for lack of knowledge." What is urgently required is a re-examination of attitudes, of the wounding contempt which the Jews have for the Arabs, and the hysterical hatred which the Arabs have for the Jews. Israel has undoubtedly the right to exist, a right which is absolute and inalienable, since it is now a fact, but it is not the right to wage a preventive war every ten years, or even the right to exist in a vacuum. Israel is surrounded by people, the Arab people, and they have a right to dignity and respect, to our sympathy and understanding, and very often to our admiration. Either to seek to destroy the State of Israel, or to neglect or decry the Arabs, is to make disaster certain. Israel exists, but the Arabs are unquestionably and overwhelmingly the people of the Middle East, and in the last resort peace can be assured only with their consent.

However, so profound a re-examination demands time, and I must leave you, I fear, with this question: Do you imagine for one moment that time is indeed to be given to men to make this re-examination?

NOTES

[1] Niebuhr, Reinhold, "David and Goliath." (*Christianity and Crisis,* Vol XXVII, No. 11, June 26, 1967, p. 141).

[2] Baly, Denis, *Multitudes in the Valley* (Seabury, 1957, p. 285).

[3] *New York Times,* August 14, 1965.

[4] *The Jewish Chronicle,* May 13, 1938.

[5] *Kongress Zeitung: Offizielles Organ des XXten Zionisten Kongress,* August 15, 1937, quoted by Nevil Barbour in *Nisi Dominus* (London: Harrap, 1946, 184, p. 306).

[6] Campbell-Johnson in *Mission with Mountbatten* (New York, E. P. Dutton, 1953, p. 203).

[7] Lacouture, Jean, "Mid-east Prognosis," *Ramparts,* Sept. 1967, p. 14.

UNITED NATIONS SECURITY COUNCIL
RESOLUTION 242 (1967)

Adopted by the Security Council
at its 1382nd meeting on 22 November 1967

The Security Council, expressing its continuing concern with the grave situation in the Middle East, *emphasizing* the inadmissibility of the acquisition of territory by war and the need to work for a just and lasting peace in which every State in the area can live in security, *emphasizing further* that all Member States in their acceptance of the Charter of the United Nations have undertaken a commitment to act in accordance with Article 2 of the Charter;

1. *Affirms* that the fulfillment of Charter principles requires the establishment of a just and lasting peace in the Middle East which should include the application of both the following principles:

    a. Withdrawal of Israeli armed forces from territories occupied in the recent conflict;

    b. Termination of all claims or states of belligerency and respect for and acknowledgement of the sovereignty, territorial integrity and political independence of every State in the area and their right to live in peace within secure and recognized boundaries free from threats or acts of force;

2. *Affirms further* the necessity:

    a. For guaranteeing freedom of navigation through international waterways in the area;

    b. For achieving a just settlement of the refugee problem;

    c. For guaranteeing the territorial inviolability and political independence of every State in the area, through measures including the establishment of demilitarized zones;

3. *Requests* the Secretary-General to designate a Special Representative to proceed to the Middle East to establish and maintain contacts with the States concerned in order to promote agreement and assist efforts to achieve a peaceful and accepted settlement in accordance with the provisions and principles in this resolution;

4. *Requests* the Secretary-General to report to the Security Council on the progress of the efforts of the Special Representative as soon as possible.